Informing the legislative debate since 1914 _____

Manufacturing Nuclear Weapon "Pits": A Decisionmaking Approach for Congress

Jonathan E. Medalia

Specialist in Nuclear Weapons Policy

August 15, 2014

Congressional Research Service

7-5700

www.crs.gov

R43685

Summary

A "pit" is the plutonium "trigger" of a thermonuclear weapon. During the Cold War, the Rocky Flats Plant (CO) made up to 2,000 pits per year (ppy), but ceased operations in 1989. Since then, the Department of Energy (DOE) has made at most 11 ppy for the stockpile, yet the Department of Defense stated that it needs DOE to have a capacity of 50 to 80 ppy to extend the life of certain weapons and for other purposes. This report focuses on 80 ppy, the upper end of this range.

Various options might reach 80 ppy. Successfully establishing pit manufacturing will require, among other things, enough laboratory space and "Material At Risk" (MAR). MAR is essentially the amount of radioactive material permitted in a building that could be released in an accident; there must be enough MAR available for manufacturing within the MAR "ceiling." PF-4, the main plutonium building at Los Alamos National Laboratory (LANL), or other structures would house manufacturing. Analytical chemistry (AC), which analyzes the composition of samples from each pit to support manufacturing, will also require availability of MAR and space.

For an option to support 80 ppy, MAR and space available for manufacturing and AC must exceed MAR and space required for 80 ppy. "Margin" is the amount by which an available amount exceeds a required amount. This report presents amounts of MAR and space potentially available for manufacturing under several options, though they may require updating. Calculation of margin—needed to determine if an option passes a minimum test for feasibility—also requires data on MAR and space required for 80 ppy, yet these data have never been calculated rigorously. As a result, it is not known if an option would increase capacity too little (making an option infeasible), too much (making an option too costly), or by an appropriate amount. Congress could direct the National Nuclear Security Administration, which operates the nuclear weapons program, to provide data on space and MAR required to manufacture 80 ppy. These data would permit calculation of space margin and MAR margin as static numbers. However, the situation is dynamic: uncertainties may materialize over time, increasing or decreasing margin.

AC poses different issues. It is needed to support production. It requires much space but uses little MAR. The nuclear weapons complex has ample excess space and MAR available for AC, so margin is not at issue, though such factors as logistics might become an issue.

Thus, three key decisions face Congress in deciding how to produce 80 ppy:

- **Decision 1:** For pit manufacturing, is there currently enough margin for space and MAR in PF-4? If not, what can be done to provide it?

- **Decision 2:** Once enough margin for space and margin for MAR are provided for pit manufacturing, what steps can be taken to maintain these margins over decades in the face of uncertainties?

- **Decision 3:** How much AC should be done at LANL, what is needed to make the space and MAR at LANL sufficient to support that amount of AC, and how much, if any, AC should be done at other sites?

Choosing among options also requires data on how options compare on cost and other metrics, setting up a process for downselection.

This report is best viewed in color, as it contains many multicolored graphics.

Contents

Background 1

    Terminology 3

        Tasks 4

        Terms 4

        Buildings 5

    An Approach to Decisionmaking 5

        Quantification of Margins and Uncertainties (QMU) 6

        Maintaining Margin by Developing Means to Offset Uncertainties 6

Requirements for Pit Manufacturing 10

    Space Options for PF-4 11

        Making More Space Available Through Major Construction 12

        Increasing Space Margin Without Major Construction 16

    MAR Options for PF-4 17

        Making More MAR Available Through Major Construction 17

        Increasing MAR Margin Without Major Construction 22

Options for Analytical Chemistry 23

    A New NNSA Path Forward on Analytical Chemistry 25

Decisions Require Data 27

Questions That Can Only Be Answered with Data 29

    Questions Requiring Data on MAR and Space 29

    Questions Requiring Data on Cost 30

Conclusion 30

Figures

Figure 1. Uncertainties May Alter Space and MAR Required and Available for Pit
    Manufacturing over Decades 8

Figure 2. Space Allocation in PF-4 12

Figure 3. Releasing Space in PF-4 by Using Two Modules 13

Figure 4. Releasing Space in PF-4 by Moving Pu-238 Work Offsite 14

Figure 5. PF-4 Roof Showing Drag Strut 22

Figure 6. Preparing a Sample for an Analytical Chemistry Instrument 23

Figure 7. Analytical Chemistry: Requirements and Options 24

Figure 8. Notional Decision Sequence for Downselecting Pit Manufacturing Options 28

Tables

Table 1. PF-4 MAR by Program 17

Table 2. PF-4 MAR with Seismic Upgrades 18

Table 3. PF-4 MAR with Two Modules 20

Table 4. PF-4 MAR with One Module...21

Appendixes

Appendix. Plutonium Tasks in PF-4 32

Contacts

Author Contact Information..33
Acknowledgments 33

Background

Congress has been deeply involved for decades in setting policy, providing funding, and supporting or rejecting programs for the nuclear weapons enterprise. For example, it established the National Nuclear Security Administration (NNSA), a semi-autonomous component of the Department of Energy (DOE) that manages the nuclear weapons program; established the Nuclear Weapons Council, a joint NNSA-Department of Defense (DOD) agency that coordinates nuclear weapons programs; rejected a major facility to manufacture a key nuclear weapon component; initiated and later rejected the Reliable Replacement Warhead; and directed NNSA, the Government Accountability Office, and others to conduct studies on nuclear weapon issues.

One issue of longstanding concern to Congress is the production of "pits." A pit is a nuclear weapon component, a hollow plutonium shell that is imploded with conventional explosives to create a nuclear explosion that triggers the rest of the weapon. While U.S. policy is not to build new-design nuclear weapons for new missions, some argue that the capacity to manufacture new pits may be needed to extend the service life of certain existing weapons, to replace pits in deployed weapons that develop pit problems unexpectedly, and to hedge against possible geopolitical surprises.

During the Cold War, the Rocky Flats Plant (CO) manufactured as many as 2,000 pits per year (ppy). On June 6, 1989, armed agents from the Federal Bureau of Investigation and the Environmental Protection Agency raided Rocky Flats to investigate suspected environmental crimes.[1] As a result, DOE first suspended pit production at Rocky Flats later that year, subsequently halted it permanently, and eventually dismantled the plant and remediated the site.

With Rocky Flats closed, Congress and the Administration searched for many years for a way to make pits. NNSA proposed a two-track strategy. In one track, Plutonium Facility 4 (PF-4), the main plutonium building at Los Alamos National Laboratory (LANL) (NM), would house a pilot plant to develop pit production processes and manufacture a small number of pits. It took until 2007 for LANL to make its first "war reserve" pits, i.e., those certified for use in the stockpile. In that year, LANL made 11 such pits, the highest number since 1989.[2]

The second track involved a facility with the capacity to make pits on an industrial scale, on the order of 100 or more ppy. Several facilities were proposed, as described in "A Sisyphean History: Failed Efforts to Construct a Building to Restore Pit Production," in CRS Report R43406, *U.S. Nuclear Weapon "Pit" Production Options for Congress*. None came to fruition. For example, in the FY2006 budget cycle, Congress eliminated funding for the Modern Pit Facility, which was to have a capacity between 125 and 450 ppy, and in its FY2013 budget request the Administration "deferred" a facility that would have conducted operations in support of pit production "for at least five years." That facility appears unlikely to proceed. Indeed, PF-4, which opened for operations in 1978, is the last U.S. plutonium processing building to come online.

---

[1] "Feds Raided Rocky Flats 25 Years Ago, Signaling the End of an Era," by Electa Draper, Denver Post, June 1, 2014, http://www.denverpost.com/news/ci_25874064/feds-raided-rocky-flats-25-years-ago-signaling.

[2] Information provided by Los Alamos National Laboratory, email, November 13, 2013.

As of June 2014, NNSA had the *capacity* to manufacture about 10 non-war reserve pits per year in PF-4. (War reserve (WR) pits are those judged acceptable for use in the nuclear stockpile. Other pits are manufactured for such purposes as development or process qualification.) However, with most work at PF-4 halted in June 2013, the actual manufacturing *rate* in June 2014 was zero for pits of any type; work is resuming at the end of June 2014. Further, the *capacity* to manufacture WR pits was zero: since there was no requirement to manufacture WR pits, some processes needed to certify pits as WR had been suspended after the previous WR build of W88 pits was completed in FY2011. NNSA anticipates manufacturing a few pits a year in the near future to prepare to manufacture WR pits.

The schedule for ramping up pit production is uncertain. A Department of Defense (DOD) official stated in 2013 that "there is no daylight between the Department of Energy and the Department of Defense on the need for both a near-term pit manufacturing capacity of 10 to 20 and then 30 by 2021, and then in the longer term for a capacity of 50 to 80 per year."[3] Also in 2013, a National Nuclear Security Administration (NNSA) document stated, "Preliminary plans call for pit production of potentially up to 80 pits per year starting as early as FY 2030."[4] In 2014, an NNSA document changed the date for achieving a 30-ppy capacity to "by 2026,"[5] and a 2014 Department of Energy (DOE) document stated, "Current plans call for pit production capability of 50-80 pits per year by FY 2030."[6] Also, Section 3114 of the FY2015 defense authorization bill, H.R. 4435, as passed by the House, would require NNSA to produce 30 WR pits per year during 2023, at least 50 during 2026, and to demonstrate for at least 90 days during 2027 the ability to manufacture WR pits at a rate of 80 per year.

Some favor a capacity of greater than 80 ppy, while others argue that a lower number would suffice.[7] That debate is beyond the scope of this report, which focuses on how to achieve a capacity of 80 ppy because that is the high end of DOD's range. While 80 ppy has been beyond reach for a quarter-century, the debate over that capacity would take on added salience to the extent that it moves within the realm of feasibility.

Congress remains deeply involved in efforts to increase pit production capacity. As noted above, Section 3114 of H.R. 4435, the FY2015 defense authorization bill as passed by the House, sets a schedule for production of WR pits. Section 3133 directs NNSA to submit "a report containing an analysis of using or modifying existing facilities across the nuclear security enterprise" to support NNSA's plutonium strategy. In its report on S. 2410, the FY2015 defense authorization bill, the Senate Armed Services Committee directed NNSA to include construction of modules (described

---

[3] Testimony of Andrew Weber, Assistant Secretary of Defense for Nuclear, Chemical, and Biological Defense Programs, in U.S. Congress. Senate. Committee on Armed Services. Subcommittee on Strategic Forces. *Hearing to Receive Testimony on Nuclear Forces and Policies in Review of the Defense Authorization Request for Fiscal Year 2014 and the Future Years Defense Program*, April 17, 2013, p. 15.

[4] U.S. Department of Energy. National Nuclear Security Administration. *Fiscal Year 2014 Stockpile Stewardship and Management Plan*, Report to Congress, June 2013, page 2-22. NNSA is the separately-organized component of the Department of Energy that is responsible for operating the U.S. nuclear weapon program.

[5] U.S. Department of Energy. Office of Chief Financial Officer. *FY 2015 Congressional Budget Request*. Volume 1, National Nuclear Security Administration, DOE/CF-0096, March 2014, p. 64, http://www.energy.gov/sites/prod/files/2014/03/f12/Volume_1_NNSA.pdf.

[6] U.S. Department of Energy. *Fiscal Year 2015 Stockpile Stewardship and Management Plan*, report to Congress, April 2014, page 2-6, http://nnsa.energy.gov/sites/default/files/nnsa/04-14-inlinefiles/2014-04-11%20FY15SSMP_FINAL_4-10-2014.pdf.

[7] For detail on these arguments, see the section "Pit Production Capacity: How Much Is Needed?," in CRS Report R43406, *U.S. Nuclear Weapon "Pit" Production Options for Congress*, by Jonathan E. Medalia

---

later), which would support an exit from a 1950s-era plutonium building at LANL by 2019, as a separate line item in the FY2016 budget "to add additional visibility into the process."[8] The House Appropriations Committee recommended a substantial increase in funding "for a robust experimental effort in fiscal year 2015 to better understand the properties of plutonium and ensure the NNSA can support certification requirements for pit reuse as an option for future [nuclear weapon life extension programs]."[9] Use of retired pits in life extension programs would reduce the number of new pits that would have to be manufactured. The committee also recommended $35.7 million for moving certain activities out of the Chemistry and Metallurgy Research building (described below), which became operational in 1952.

While DOD has a requirement for up to 80 ppy, some key questions about *how* to manufacture at that rate remain not only unanswered but also unasked. These questions involve details about the facilities at LANL and perhaps elsewhere that would fabricate pits and perform supporting tasks. Without answers to these questions, Congress cannot know whether existing buildings, without modifications, could manufacture 80 ppy; or if modest upgrades would suffice; or if major construction would be needed to augment capacity. This report provides a framework for analyzing requirements for manufacturing, details key questions, and raises the possibility that Congress may choose to direct NNSA to generate the data needed to answer them.

Specifically, regardless of what capacity is needed, and when, Congress and the Administration will need to decide among options. This report presents three key decisions and an approach to help structure them. It focuses on two metrics: the amount of two facility resources (laboratory floor space and Material At Risk (MAR), discussed next) available for pit manufacturing. It shows that it is not known whether available amounts suffice. While NNSA has extrapolated space and MAR requirements for manufacturing 80 ppy from much lower numbers, extrapolations set an upper bound and would overstate requirements. As such, they are of questionable value for decisionmaking. Space and MAR requirements for manufacturing 80 ppy have never been calculated rigorously, though they could be. Comparing space and MAR required vs. available would show whether there is enough space and MAR at the moment. Over time, however, various factors will affect availability and requirements. While few of these factors can be predicted, this report discusses ways to offset any adverse effects from them. In addition, decisions will be needed regarding analytical chemistry, which supports pit manufacturing. For background, see CRS Report R43406, *U.S. Nuclear Weapon "Pit" Production Options for Congress;* CRS Report R43428, *U.S. Nuclear Weapon "Pit" Production: Background and Options in Brief,* is a condensed version.

Terminology

Several tasks, terms, and buildings are central to the subsequent discussion.

---

[8] U.S. Congress, Senate Committee on Armed Services, *Carl Levin National Defense Authorization Act for Fiscal Year 2015*, Report to accompany S. 2410, 113th Cong., 2nd sess., June 2, 2014, S.Rept. 113-176 (Washington: GPO, 2014), p. 289.

[9] U.S. Congress, House Committee on Appropriations, *Energy and Water Development Appropriations Bill, 2015*, Report to accompany H.R. 4923, 113th Cong., 2nd sess., June 20, 2013, H.Rept. 113-486 (Washington: GPO, 2014), p. 131.

Tasks

- **Pit manufacturing** involves several tasks. Among other things, pit *fabrication* casts "hemishells" (half-pits) of plutonium, machines them to remove excess material, and welds two together to form a pit. The current pit fabrication line was intended as a pilot plant; its capacity is about 10 ppy. It is being upgraded to reach a capacity of 30 ppy; further upgrades would be needed to reach 80. Pit *manufacturing* also involves such supporting tasks as purifying plutonium for use in pits; certification to ensure that finished pits meet required standards; material control and accountability; waste management; and analytical chemistry. This report uses "fabrication" as a subset of "manufacturing."

- **Analytical chemistry** (AC) is essential for pit manufacturing, but this report considers it separately because it has large space requirements. AC analyzes plutonium samples taken from each pit at various stages in its fabrication. AC determines the isotopic composition of the plutonium and the amount of alloying materials and impurities it contains. Pit fabrication requires extensive AC for every pit. AC supports other pit manufacturing tasks, and non-pit tasks as well, though historically pit fabrication has been the greatest user of AC. The building at Los Alamos National Laboratory (LANL) that currently performs AC to support pit manufacture and many other plutonium tasks is in poor shape and not seismically robust. DOE wants to halt work there by 2019, so one or more other facilities will be needed.

Terms

- **Laboratory floor space**, or "space." Laboratory buildings have space for corridors, offices, etc., but laboratory floor space is where AC, pit fabrication, and other work is done. Space is expressed in units of square feet (sf).

- **"Material At Risk"** (MAR) is "the amount of radioactive materials ... available to be acted on by a given physical stress."[10] It is material that could be released by a disaster, such as an earthquake that collapses a building followed by a fire. Each building that works with plutonium has a building-specific MAR allowance. MAR is expressed in units of plutonium equivalent, discussed next.

- **Plutonium** is the fissile material in pits. Four forms are relevant here. *Plutonium-239* (Pu-239) is the fissile isotope in pits. However, pits contain other plutonium isotopes in addition to Pu-239; that mixture is called *weapons-grade plutonium* (WGPu). Since some of the other isotopes are more radioactive than Pu-239, WGPu is about 1.5 times as radioactive as Pu-239. *Plutonium-238* (Pu-238) is 277 times more radioactive than Pu-239. It is used to power space probes and has some military applications, but is not used in pits. It is relevant to pit manufacturing options because 40 percent of the MAR allowance in PF-4 is allocated to Pu-238.[11] Moving some or all Pu-238 work out of PF-4, the main

---

[10] U.S. Department of Energy. DOE Handbook: *Airborne Release Fractions/Rates and Respirable Fractions for Nonreactor Nuclear Facilities,* Vol. I, Analysis of Experimental Data, DOE-HDBK-3010-94, December 1994, p. xix.

[11] Information provided by Los Alamos National Laboratory, October 23, 2013. Note that MAR *allowance* for a program must at all times be greater than or equal to the actual MAR that the program is using.

plutonium building at LANL, would make MAR and space available for other purposes. In PF-4, MAR is measured in units of *plutonium equivalent* (PE), which is about 1.38 times as radioactive as Pu-239; this measure is linked to potential dose if plutonium is released, such as by an earthquake and fire.

Buildings

- **PF-4** (Plutonium Facility 4) is the only building in the United States with the combination of attributes required to make pits: high security, pit fabrication equipment, and the ability to handle high-MAR processes. Its current MAR allowance is 1,800 kg PE. It is located at LANL, the nation's "center of excellence" for plutonium, and the only place that has made pits since 1989; as a result, LANL has the scientific, engineering, and craft expertise needed to make pits. PF-4 also performs other tasks involving plutonium. It is the last U.S. plutonium processing facility to be brought online, in 1978, and is the only remaining U.S. multi-program, multi-function plutonium processing facility. It would be about a half-century old when production is anticipated to reach 80 ppy. Within LANL, PF-4 is located in Technical Area (TA) 55.

- The **Chemistry and Metallurgy Research** (CMR) building currently provides AC support for limited pit manufacture and other plutonium tasks in PF-4. Most of it was completed in 1952. It is "genuinely decrepit" [12] and "structurally unsound," [13] in the words of two studies, and is much more vulnerable to collapse in an earthquake than more recent buildings. [14] Accordingly, "NNSA maintains its commitment to cease programmatic operations in the CMR facility at LANL in approximately 2019." [15]

- The **Radiological Laboratory-Utility-Office Building** (RLUOB, pronounced "rulob") was completed in FY2010. It is configured for AC. NNSA plans that RLUOB would house AC equipment needed to support pit manufacture, and possibly enough to support manufacture of 80 ppy.

An Approach to Decisionmaking

An approach to maintaining confidence in nuclear weapons may help provide lessons for decisionmaking on pits. This section describes that approach, then modifies it to make it applicable to pits.

---

[12] William Perry et al., *America's Strategic Posture*, Congressional Commission on the Strategic Posture of the United States, Washington, United States Institute for Peace Press, 2009, p. 50.

[13] Defense Nuclear Facilities Safety Board, "Summary of Significant Safety-Related Infrastructure Issues at Operating Defense Nuclear Facilities," letter report to the Congress, September 10, 2010, p. 1, http://www.dnfsb.gov/sites/default/files/Board%20Activities/Reports/Reports%20to%20Congress/2010/sr_2010910_4673.pdf.

[14] For example, Michael Salmon, structural engineer and seismic analyst, Los Alamos National Laboratory, estimates that "collapsing RLUOB [a building completed in FY2010, described below] would take an earthquake with 4 to 12 times more force than an earthquake that would collapse CMR." Information provided December 2013.

[15] U.S. Department of Energy. Office of Chief Financial Officer. *FY 2015 Congressional Budget Request*, Volume 1, National Nuclear Security Administration, DOE/CF-0096, March 2014, p. 213, http://www.energy.gov/sites/prod/files/2014/03/f12/Volume_1_NNSA.pdf.

Quantification of Margins and Uncertainties (QMU)

In 1992, the United States began a moratorium on nuclear testing that continues to the present.[16] Concurrent with the moratorium, the United States developed and implemented a stockpile stewardship program to maintain nuclear weapons without testing. An issue became how to demonstrate confidence in the safety and reliability of these weapons. One approach, developed by LANL and Lawrence Livermore National Laboratory (LLNL), was Quantification of Margins and Uncertainties, or QMU.[17] The idea underlying QMU was that several steps in a nuclear weapon—transmission of a signal to detonate the weapon, explosion of the high explosive surrounding the pit, transmission of the energy from the explosion of the primary stage to the secondary stage, and detonation of the secondary stage—must all work for the weapon to function.[18] Each step, or "gate" in QMU terminology, can be quantified. For example, a certain amount of energy must be transmitted to the secondary for it to detonate. Another QMU concept is margin. If the minimum amount of energy needed to detonate the secondary is X, and the amount of energy predicted to be transmitted to the secondary is 3X, then there is a margin of 2X, i.e., margin is the amount by which the predicted quantity exceeds the minimum required quantity. At the same time, there are uncertainties in the predicted quantity. Did the calculation incorporate all relevant variables? Were there biases in experiments on which the calculations were based? Were the most relevant nuclear tests used as a data source? The uncertainty can be quantified through calculations (such as computer models); further, the amount of uncertainty is bounded because each gate has an upper and a lower limit. If margin exceeds uncertainty for a particular gate, then there can be confidence that the weapon will "pass through" that gate satisfactorily, and if margin exceeds uncertainty for all gates, there can be confidence that the weapon will work. The degree of confidence at each gate is expressed as margin divided by uncertainty; the higher the number, the greater the confidence.

Maintaining Margin by Developing Means to Offset Uncertainties

QMU provides three key concepts relevant to decisionmaking on pit manufacturing.

- **Margin,** in this case, is the amount by which (1) space available for pit manufacturing exceeds (2) space required to manufacture 80 ppy, and the amount by which (3) MAR available for pit manufacturing exceeds (4) MAR required to manufacture 80 ppy. (The two margins are independent.) Thus, solving for margin requires four numbers. Figures 1-7 show items (1) and (3) under various scenarios. Regarding items (2) and (4), LANL has examined space and MAR needed to fabricate 80 ppy in a preliminary fashion, but has not performed a detailed analysis of the full pit manufacturing process, including plutonium supply, waste management, AC, external support activities, and fabrication.[19] To enable calculation of margin, Congress would need to obtain two numbers:

---

[16] This report uses "nuclear testing" to mean underground nuclear explosions producing a nuclear yield. Other tests are done to nuclear weapons, their materials, and components that do not involve a nuclear yield.

[17] For a detailed discussion of QMU, see National Research Council, Division on Engineering and Physical Sciences, committee on the Evaluation of Quantification of Margins and Uncertainties Methodology for Assessing and Certifying the Reliability of the Nuclear Stockpile, *Evaluation of Quantification of Margins and Uncertainties: Methodology for Assessing and Certifying the Reliability of the Nuclear Stockpile,* Washington, National Academies Press, 2009, 79 p.

[18] The primary stage consists of the pit, high explosives, and other materials. Its detonation sets off the secondary stage.

[19] Information provided by Los Alamos National Laboratory, April 29, 2014.

- Space required to manufacture 80 ppy, and

- MAR required to manufacture 80 ppy.

In addition, available space and MAR figures would probably need to be updated. Once those numbers are provided, Congress would be in a better position to determine which options would free enough space and MAR in PF-4 to manufacture 80 ppy, or if there is already sufficient space and MAR in PF-4. LANL (and perhaps other sites) has computer models and other resources needed to perform these calculations. AC also has space and MAR requirements but, as discussed in "Options for Analytical Chemistry," margins are not at issue because the nuclear weapons complex has ample space and MAR for AC for 80 ppy.

- **Uncertainty:** Margins can change over time. While MAR and space margins could be calculated precisely for the present moment, they cannot be calculated in advance because many actions, events, decisions, and discoveries have the potential to create uncertainties that could increase or decrease availability of, or requirements for, space and MAR, thus increasing or decreasing margin. **Figure 1** shows hypothetical examples of uncertainties: those in red could reduce margin, and those in green could increase it. The longer the timeframe, the more uncertainties can be expected to emerge. While the *effects* of these uncertainties on pit manufacturing can be calculated once they materialize, the *likelihood* that they will come into being, and even the type of uncertainties—in contrast to the uncertainties in QMU—cannot be predicted or bounded, let alone quantified. Another means of maintaining margin, not shown in **Figure 1**, is for Congress or NNSA to bar from PF-4 new missions that would consume MAR and space, especially those that could be placed elsewhere.

- **Maintaining margin despite uncertainties:** It would not be acceptable to let uncertainties that materialize into actual events reduce margin below zero, as that could force a halt to pit manufacturing. One way to maintain enough margin to support a specified pit manufacturing capacity in the face of uncertainties is to develop multiple means to counterbalance uncertainties that would reduce margin. Some means could be implemented promptly; others could be developed, held in reserve, and implemented only as needed. Having these means available for future deployment would add confidence that sufficient margin could be maintained.

Figure 1. Uncertainties May Alter Space and MAR Required and Available for Pit Manufacturing over Decades

Hypothetical Actions, Events, Decisions, and Discoveries Could Reduce or Increase Margin in PF-4

	Factors	Example 1	Example 2	Example 3	Example 4
1	Factors increasing supply (availability) of MAR	Develop and install means to increase PF-4 seismic resilience	Clean out PF-4 vault, store more plutonium needed for ongoing work in vault	Remove unneeded plutonium	New interpretation of a regulation permits increased MAR (as with RLUOB)
2	Factors reducing supply (availability) of MAR	A previously unknown seismic fault is discovered at TA-55	New interpretation of a regulation tightens restrictions	Cracks in concrete from an earthquake reduce confidence in PF-4	Defense Nuclear Facilities Safety Board raises concerns about an existing procedure
3	Factors increasing supply (availability) of space	More efficient use is made of PF-4 basement; some lab operations are moved there	Build modules	Clean out and repurpose rooms in PF-4	Add shielding around gloveboxes, permitting more in a room
4	Factors reducing supply (availability) of space	Add non-pit mission in PF-4	Pit manufacture uses more equipment than previously thought	A new regulation requires increasing space between gloveboxes to reduce dose	Contamination from an accident prevents use of a room in PF-4 for some time
5	Factors increasing demand (requirements) for MAR	Requirement changed to 125 ppy because of geopolitical developments	Faster process exposes more MAR	Partial collapse shuts CMR; its plutonium is moved to PF-4	Problem in a deployed weapon brings more pits to PF-4 for analysis
6	Factors reducing demand (requirements) for MAR	Requirement changed to 40 ppy because pit reuse proves more applicable than expected	Place more plutonium in highly robust containers	Develop lower-MAR manufacturing processes	Move Pu-238 mission out of PF-4
7	Factors increasing demand (requirements) for space	Requirement changed to 125 ppy because pit surveillance reveals unexpected pit problems	Workload for processing drums containing plutonium waste increases abruptly	A new manufacturing layout increases through-put but uses more space	Pit Disassembly and Conversion workload increases
8	Factors reducing demand (requirements) for space	Requirement changed to 40 ppy because plutonium is found to age more slowly than previously thought	Use 2 or 3 shifts per day	A new layout that minimizes space is designed	Some AC equipment is moved from PF-4 to RLUOB

Source: CRS.

Notes: Green boxes, factors increasing margin; red boxes, factors reducing margin.

Determining how much MAR and space would be needed to manufacture 80 ppy would require an industrial process analysis. A study would seek to determine what equipment would be needed to manufacture 80 ppy; lay out production lines in PF-4 to accommodate that equipment while retaining space needed for other tasks; determine what tasks, if any, could be moved from PF-4 if necessary to accommodate the lines; and calculate what MAR would result from this production line configuration. An extrapolation provides an upper bound: LANL is planning to increase PF-

4's capacity to 30 ppy, and if a given amount of space and equipment can make 30 ppy, then three times those amounts could make 90 ppy. However, such a study is likely to find that less space and equipment would suffice because of efficiencies. In a process step, for example, a piece of equipment that could support manufacture of 300 ppy would suffice for any number less than 300, whether 10, 30, or 80. A study would need to take into account that there are many ways to make more space or MAR available and to reduce space or MAR requirements, thereby increasing margin, as discussed under "Space Options for PF-4" and "MAR Options for PF-4." This detailed analysis would be needed to determine whether enough MAR allowance and space could be made available in PF-4 to manufacture 80 ppy. Given that margin can change over time, it might be useful to have an annual review of margin and potential factors that could affect it.

Which organization could perform such a study? Candidates include LANL, another lab or plant in the nuclear weapons complex, NNSA, DOD, or an independent group like the National Academy of Sciences or the JASON defense advisory group. Since LANL is intimately familiar with PF-4, it could be argued that it should do the report. On the other hand, LANL could be perceived as having a conflict of interest. An independent group would not have this potential conflict of interest but would not have LANL's knowledge of PF-4. To address this dilemma, LANL might conduct the initial study and an independent group could review it. Another approach would be to have the study prepared jointly by LANL and Lawrence Livermore National Laboratory (LLNL), or prepared by LANL and peer-reviewed by LLNL. LANL and LLNL are both nuclear weapon design laboratories, so LLNL's expertise would be of use in evaluating a LANL study. Since the two labs have often competed for projects and have a reputation as "friendly adversaries," involving LLNL would provide an added measure of confidence in the study.

Before the study could begin, the Nuclear Weapons Council would need to define key parameters:

- What capacity is being sought? Is it 80 ppy, or 50 with a surge capacity to 80, or 80 with a surge capacity to 125, or something else?

- What operating tempo is planned? Would manufacturing use 1 shift per day/5 days a week, 2 shifts per day/5 days a week, or operate 24/7? The answer is related to capacity. If the capacity sought is 80 ppy using 3 shifts per day, a higher surge capacity would be difficult at best. The answer is also related to cost and equipment. Using two shifts per day, it might be possible to reach 80 ppy with equipment that would support 50 ppy on a single shift; a more costly option would be to increase the amount of equipment (and thus floor space used) to enable production of 80 with a single shift.

- Would the capacity be held in standby mode most of the time, available for use as needed; operated for months or years at 80 ppy for certain pit campaigns and held in low-rate production mode for other periods; operated at a steady rate, less than 80, to level out the workload between periods when no pits are needed and periods when 80 ppy are needed; or operated at full capacity at all times?

- What programs could be moved out of PF-4 if necessary to create enough space or MAR, where would they go, what would the move cost, and who would pay?

- What is a reasonable tradeoff between cost and capacity? As a notional example, if LANL could manufacture 70 ppy using existing buildings and an operating cost of $500 million per year, but it would cost $2 billion for new construction and $700 million in annual operating cost to manufacture 80 ppy, would the added capacity be worth the added cost? A sensitivity analysis would provide the data, but the answer would be a matter of judgment.

- It appears that it would take over a decade to reach 80 ppy, and the path to that capacity is obscure. If the path becomes clearer, it would become more important to determine if 80 is the right number, or if it should be higher or lower.

This report starts with a static approach to pit manufacturing, examining the space and MAR margins for 80 ppy once current projects in PF-4 that will increase permitted MAR and make more space available are completed. This static approach provides a baseline and metrics to indicate whether margin is ample, minimal, or insufficient, and to judge the impact of future deviations from this baseline. Next, the report takes a dynamic approach, noting that uncertainties could affect margin and how they might be offset. Finally, it considers analytical chemistry requirements. This approach leads to three decisions Congress may choose to consider:

- **Decision 1:** For pit manufacturing, is there currently enough margin for space and MAR in PF-4? If not, what can be done to provide it?

- **Decision 2:** Once enough margin for space and margin for MAR are provided for pit manufacturing, what steps can be taken to maintain these margins over decades in the face of uncertainties?

- **Decision 3:** For AC, space and MAR available across the nuclear weapons complex exceed space and MAR required by a considerable amount, so margin is not an issue. Instead, the issue is how much AC should be done at LANL and how much, if any, AC should be done at other sites?

Requirements for Pit Manufacturing

The floor layout to manufacture 30 ppy would fully consume the space, and most of the MAR allowance, currently available in PF-4. As a result, manufacturing 80 ppy would require more space and MAR than are currently available for that task in PF-4. Further, updated seismic modeling results raised concerns that an earthquake might collapse or otherwise compromise the building,[20] forcing a reduction in PF-4 MAR from 2,600 kg PE to 1,800 kg PE. However, LANL is undertaking several projects that would increase the MAR permitted in PF-4. Various projects

---

[20] "In public comments at a Capitol Hill Club event this summer [2013], DNFSB member Jack Mansfield explained the Board's concerns. The [PF-4] facility, built in the late 1970s, is 'brittle,' Mansfield said. 'It was discovered after this facility was built that large buildings, to be survivable in serious earthquakes, have to have a bit of ductility. It was also discovered after the Loma Prieta earthquake that round columns, if accelerated up into the plywood they support, crumble. Those two vulnerabilities were identified early, but they're not built into PF-4.'

"He added: 'The result is that there is a probability, albeit small, that the building could collapse, with great loss of life within and with dispersal of plutonium.' Previous upgrades were based on calculations that did not fully characterize the problems facing the facility, Mansfield said. Those calculations were 'very good' and 'did a lot,' Mansfield said, but 'the problem is that any of the columns, crushed like the ones on the highway did—the whole roof would go down like a zipper.'" Todd Jacobson, "DOE Says Alternate Analysis of PF-4 Seismic Risks Will Be Done in Dec.," *Nuclear Weapons & Materials Monitor,* September 6, 2013, http://www.lasg.org/press/2013/NWMM_6Sep2013.html.

Also, the Defense Nuclear Facilities Safety Board (DNFSB) stated: "DOE and the National Nuclear Security Administration (NNSA) have made progress in addressing a number of these [seismic] safety issues, but the Board remains concerned that PF-4 is vulnerable to seismic collapse for the seismic hazard at LANL." Letter from DNFSB to the Congress of the United States, July 15, 2013, http://www.dnfsb.gov/sites/default/files/Board%20Activities/Reports/Reports%20to%20Congress/qr__22406.pdf.

---

to increase seismic robustness have been underway for years; see the section "Increasing MAR Margin Without Major Construction." They proceed on an open-ended basis guided by results of continuing analyses. Once some additional upgrades are completed, PF-4's MAR allowance may revert to 2,600 kg or perhaps some other number. This analysis assumes a MAR allowance of 2,600 kg PE and, as noted in the sidebar, uses space data from 2012.

LANL points out that PF-4, as the only U.S. building that is currently able to make pits, is essential to the entire nuclear weapons enterprise: no PF-4, no pits, no LEPs that require new pits. PF-4 is limited in space and MAR. The MAR limit is somewhat flexible, as various measures can increase it. Similarly, space within PF-4 may be shifted from one purpose to another, and LANL is undertaking such projects, e.g., decontaminating some rooms in PF-4 that are no longer in use and "repurposing" them to make them available for pit manufacture or other uses. However, the space limit is absolute: 60,000 sf of laboratory space. If manufacturing 80 ppy requires more space than is available in PF-4, NNSA would need to find alternatives, whether building modules, moving some tasks to other sites, or reducing capacity to whatever the available space could accommodate.

> **Which MAR and Space Data to Use?**
>
> Space available in PF-4 changes from year to year. A project may be completed, so its rooms may become available; a project may consolidate space, making one of several rooms available; another project may need to add a new instrument or process, requiring more space; or a project may increase or decrease its throughput, altering its MAR. **Figure 2** uses space data provided by LANL for PF-4 as of early 2012, while **Figure 3** and **Figure 4** show options that modify space usage. Actual MAR changes from hour to hour, depending on which operations are in progress. Most operations in PF-4 were suspended in June 2013 and as of mid-June 2014 had not fully resumed. **Table 1**, which also uses data supplied by LANL, shows MAR used by programs on February 27, 2013, i.e., before the suspension. Future MAR and space numbers are likely to differ from those presented here. Different numbers would produce different results in terms of which options are feasible, but would not alter the analytic approach of this report.

It would be difficult for Congress to decide how to obtain the space and MAR for manufacturing 80 ppy without knowing whether there will be sufficient MAR and space margins for 80 ppy. This section considers options that might make the needed space and MAR available. Note that while margin must always be greater than zero, the amount of available space and MAR needed to maintain margin could expand or contract depending on whether required space and MAR expand or contract. For example, MAR insufficient for 80 ppy might suffice for 40 ppy.

Space Options for PF-4

Various options could make more space available in PF-4 for pit manufacture. Some might require major construction; others might not. Sufficient space to manufacture 80 ppy might even be readily available within PF-4 with little or no work. Options would vary in terms of their projected cost and schedule. Some might be implemented quickly and at low cost; others might take longer and cost more. Still others that would entail high cost and long leadtime could be studied (e.g., design work on modules) to determine whether they are feasible and, if so, to facilitate possible future deployment. Any option could be deployed promptly or held in reserve. Thus, for each, a decision would be needed on whether to proceed and, if so, when. Such decisions would depend on how much space was needed given then-current space availability and, later, on the extent of any reduction in space margin. This analysis also applies to "MAR Options for PF-4," below, and is not repeated there.

Making More Space Available Through Major Construction

Figure 2 shows the 2012 allocation of space in PF-4 by program. The gray area, 4,700 square feet (sf), is available for immediate repurposing. It consists of laboratory rooms not currently in use. White areas represent non-laboratory space. Pit fabrication occupies 12,000 sf.

Figure 2. Space Allocation in PF-4

by Program or Activity

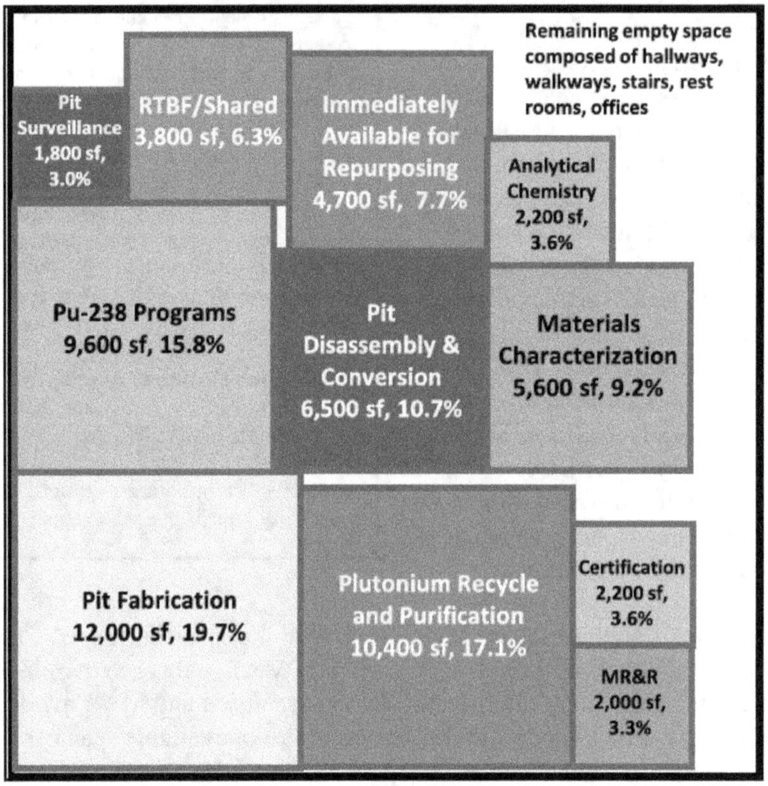

Source: Los Alamos National Laboratory.

Notes: PF-4 is approximately 280 feet on a side. The blocks in this diagram represent space allocations to scale but do not show the physical location of each activity within PF-4. Figures for square feet (sf) and percentages are for laboratory floor space. The **Appendix** describes each task shown in this and subsequent figures.

One option involves building one or more "modules," reinforced-concrete structures that would be buried near PF-4 and connected to it by a tunnel. Preliminary concepts envision that each module would be roughly 5,000 sf of laboratory space, and that modules would be designed for high-MAR tasks, such as casting plutonium into hemishells or working with Pu-238.

Figure 3 shows how moving these two tasks into two modules could release space in PF-4. It shows 5,000 sf being moved from Pu-238 programs to Module 1, with the released space used for pit manufacturing; another 5,000 sf being moved from pit fabrication space in PF-4 to Module 2, making that much more net space available for pit manufacturing; and the 4,700 sf of space immediately available for repurposing also being used for pit manufacturing, adding 14,700 sf in PF-4 and Module 2 for pit work, with pit fabrication space plus other space made available for pit manufacturing totaling 26,700 sf. (Space for some other tasks, such as Plutonium Recycle and Purification, would also support pit manufacturing.) LANL maintains that a key advantage of modules is that they would permit expansion of capacity on an as-needed basis rather than trying to build a "big box" plutonium building that would attempt to accommodate all foreseeable future needs, an approach that has been rejected for several big-box buildings over many years. Others respond that modules could be costly and, if existing buildings can be used, may not be needed.

Another option (not shown) would be to build one module for Pu-238 work or pit casting. This option would release some 5,000 sf in PF-4 in addition to the 4,700 sf available for repurposing.

Figure 3. Releasing Space in PF-4 by Using Two Modules

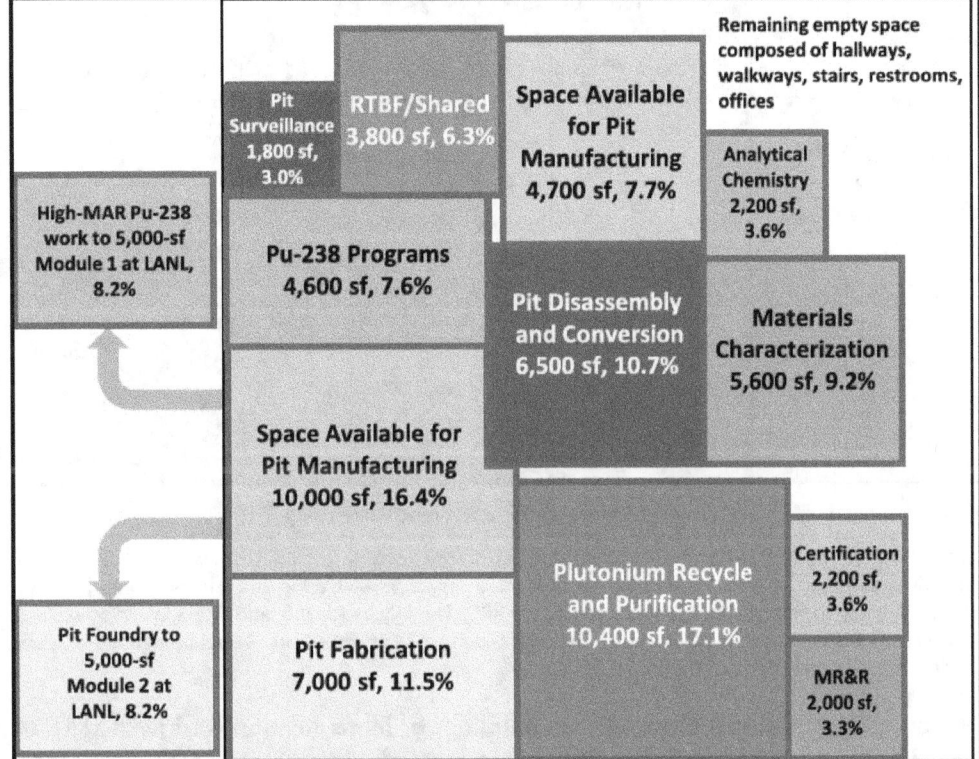

Source: Base graphic by Los Alamos National Laboratory, modifications by CRS.

Note: The blocks in this diagram represent space allocations to scale but do not show the physical location of each activity within PF-4. Modules (external to PF-4) are to same scale as PF-4.

A third option would move Pu-238 work from LANL. Two sites, Savannah River Site (SRS) (SC) and Idaho National Laboratory (INL), have worked with Pu-238 and have stated that they

have, or could modify, buildings to do this work. **Figure 4** shows this option permitting the full amount of space used for Pu-238 in PF-4, 9,600 sf, to be made available for pit manufacturing, as well as the 4,700 sf of repurposable space. This option would result in 26,300 sf for pit work in PF-4. In determining the feasibility of this option, NNSA would need to evaluate space and MAR at other sites, as well as the costs—the move itself, repurposing PF-4 space, refurbishing, reequipping, and staffing the new facility, and so on—of the move.

Figure 4. Releasing Space in PF-4 by Moving Pu-238 Work Offsite

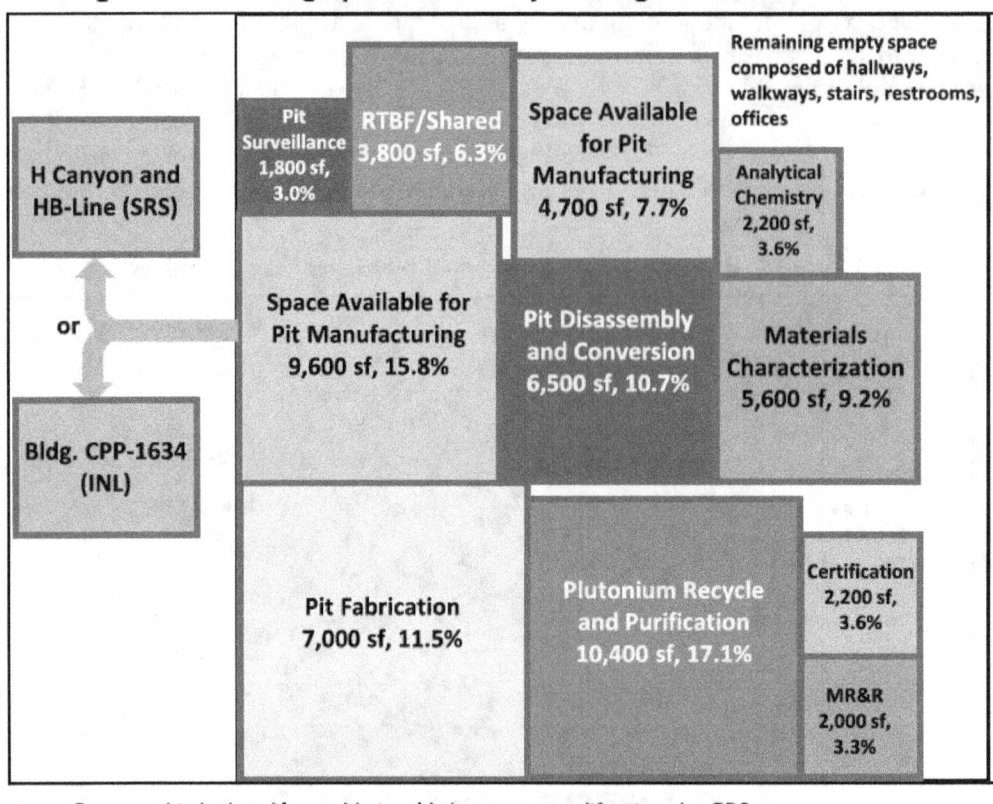

Source: Base graphic by Los Alamos National Laboratory, modifications by CRS.

Note: The blocks in this diagram represent space allocations to scale but do not show the physical location of each activity within PF-4. The space in the block labeled "Space Available for Pit Manufacturing, 9,600 sq. ft." is made available by moving all Pu-238 work to INL or SRS. The blocks for INL and SRS are not to scale, as a detailed study would be required to determine how much space at either site would be needed to accommodate activities that currently occupy 9,600 sf in PF-4.

A fourth option to release space would be to build one or more modules for lower-MAR activities now housed in PF-4, such as materials characterization, which occupies 5,600 square feet of laboratory space, and a gas gun,[21] which occupies another 1,200 square feet of lab space. Moving out these two activities would release about 6,800 square feet of PF-4 lab space, 11 percent of the total. Some waste processing activities in PF-4 are also lower-MAR. While these activities have a lower MAR level, they would still require Hazard Category 3-level facilities. LANL expects these modules would be comparable in cost to Hazard Category-2 modules.[22]

LANL calculates that the current 12,000 sf in PF-4 available for pit fabrication is enough to fabricate 30 ppy once certain upgrades have been completed.[23] However, the space needed for 80

---

[21] A gas gun shoots a metal projectile into a piece of plutonium to study how the latter behaves under impact.

[22] Information provided by Los Alamos National Laboratory, July 15, 2014. A Hazard Category (HC) refers to maximum amount of radioactive material (in this case, plutonium) a building can contain. HC-3 buildings can hold 38.6 up to 2,610 grams Pu-239 equivalent; HC-2 buildings, like PF-4, can hold 2,610 grams or more. See "Key Regulatory Terms" in CRS Report R43406, *U.S. Nuclear Weapon "Pit" Production Options for Congress*, by Jonathan E. Medalia.

[23] The current capacity of PF-4, with current equipment, is about 10 ppy. However, LANL has embarked on a series of small activities to replace and remove obsolescent equipment and in so doing to reconfigure the space to improve (continued...)

ppy would not increase linearly with capacity. Even calculating the amount of space for equipment is not linear. Each piece of equipment has a specific throughput. If one piece can support 40 ppy, then 80 ppy would require two such pieces, but if one piece suffices to support 30 ppy, then 80 ppy would require three pieces. Adding complexity to the calculation, constraints imposed by room layout, facility layout, and process flows must be considered.

Adding further complexity, determining the space needed for 80 ppy requires analyzing the entire manufacturing process, not just equipment requirements, including answers to such questions as:

- In moving to 80 ppy, how much additional space would be needed in PF-4 for supporting infrastructure, such as packaging, shipping, receiving, waste management, and temporary storage, as well as the material control and accountability needed to send hundreds if not thousands of AC samples annually to LLNL or SRS if those sites are used? Would this latter number be much reduced if the samples were all analyzed at LANL?

- What turnaround time would be required for samples moved onsite or shipped offsite? The time required to receive AC results would be needed in order to estimate the number of gloveboxes and temporary storage locations, and would thus affect space requirements. The analysis would need to take into account that most AC is done on a confirmatory basis, i.e., manufacturing proceeds on the assumption that AC results will confirm that samples are within specifications. (Hemishells not within specifications would be recycled.) Such AC is not time-sensitive. On the other hand, AC to analyze process problems requires fast turnaround to minimize the time the process is shut down. At issue: how much AC is likely to be time-sensitive?

- How much plutonium would pit fabrication need? Increasing the amount of plutonium would require adding electrorefining furnaces, increasing space requirements.

- Since the United States no longer produces plutonium, all U.S. plutonium is "old," such as from retired pits. As plutonium decays, it produces other elements, such as uranium and americium. These must be removed by chemical processes to purify plutonium for use in new pits. (Chemical processes do not remove specific isotopes of plutonium.) PF-4 uses 10,400 sf for plutonium recycle and purification. How much plutonium could that area purify per year? How many ppy would that capacity support? How much more space would be needed to provide plutonium for 80 ppy? Alternatively, could these processes be moved to another site, such as Savannah River Site?

- Pit fabrication generates some plutonium scraps, such as excess material from castings, shavings from lathes, and pits scrapped because they did not meet specifications. Providing for recycle of this plutonium requires space, and producing 80 ppy would require more space than 30. How much space would plutonium disposition require?

(...continued)

operational efficiency. These activities are intended to increase the capacity of the 12,000-sf space to 30 ppy. Information provided by Los Alamos National Laboratory, April 10, 2014.

Increasing Space Margin Without Major Construction

While major construction could make more space available, increasing efficient use of existing space could increase the space margin. This could be done in several ways, such as:

- Designing work flow to minimize space utilization. When DOE decided to move pit manufacture to PF-4, the process line was intended as a pilot plant to develop, quickly, techniques for resuming production. It was not intended as the nation's pit production site; other proposed facilities, such as the Modern Pit Facility, were to fill that role. LANL is currently redesigning the existing pit fabrication space in PF-4 to manufacture up to 30 ppy instead of 10; increased efficiencies of this type would reduce space requirements for 80 ppy, increasing margin.

- Develop equipment and processes for faster work flow so fewer pieces of equipment to manufacture a specified number of pits, reducing floor space.

- Repurpose unused space or space used for lower-priority programs, as discussed.

- Make more efficient use of PF-4's basement, which houses the nuclear materials vault and most utilities, and provides space for shipping and receiving and for staging waste drums. It may be possible to move out some operations from the basement, such as drum storage, freeing space to house such laboratory-floor operations as nondestructive analysis,[24] and some waste management operations.

- Move some equipment out of PF-4. For example, PF-4 houses a gas gun, which propels a metal slug into a plutonium target to study how plutonium behaves under impact. The gas gun uses 1,200 sf of laboratory space in PF-4, and some basement space. Moving it to RLUOB (if that building's MAR were to be increased substantially) or to another site would release space in PF-4.

- Use two or three shifts a day rather than one. So doing would make more intensive use of space by allowing fewer pieces of equipment to produce a given amount of product, thereby reducing space requirements. Rocky Flats Plant, for example, generally operated using three shifts per day. On the other hand, a higher tempo for an extended period could increase operating cost, require more maintenance, reduce time available for maintenance, increase the likelihood of equipment failure, and have more impact on production if equipment fails.

Such options would almost surely be faster and less costly than major construction, but without data on space required for 80 ppy, it is not possible to know if they would provide enough space.

---

[24] As an example of nondestructive analysis, radiation detectors can determine the amount of plutonium in a waste drum without opening the drum.

MAR Options for PF-4

Making More MAR Available Through Major Construction

As with space, there are options to provide more MAR. The total MAR allowance for PF-4 on February 27, 2013,[25] was 1,800 kg PE. **Table 1** shows the percentage of the 1,800 kg MAR.

Table 1. PF-4 MAR by Program

Units in this graphic are kilograms of plutonium, not area
MAR allowance for PF-4 for this configuration is 1,800 kg of plutonium
MAR is actual usage on February 27, 2013

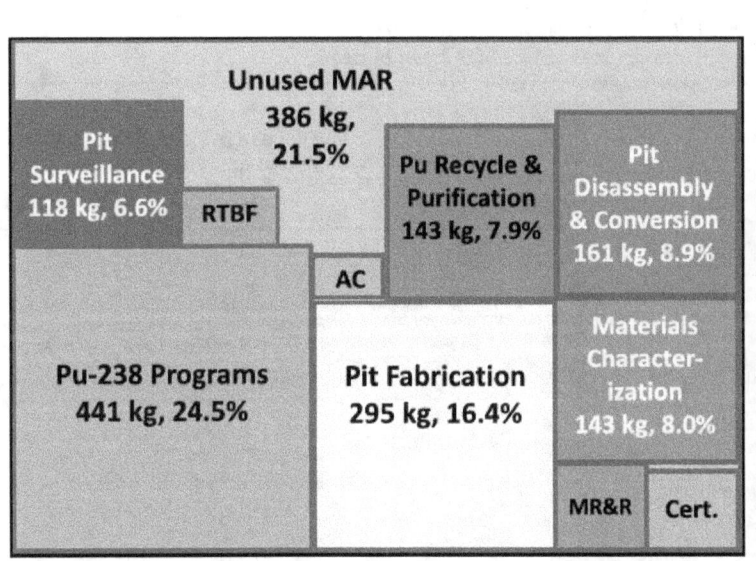

Program	MAR (kilo-grams)	Percent of PF-4 MAR allowance
PF-4		
Pit Fabrication	295	16.4
Unused MAR	386	21.5
Certification	34	1.9
Pit Surveillance	118	6.6
AC	14	0.8
MC	143	8.0
Pu-238 Programs	441	24.5
PDC	161	8.9
MR&R	38	2.1
RTBF	26	1.5
PRP	143	7.9
Total	**1,800**	**100.0**

Source: Data provided by Los Alamos National Laboratory; graphic by CRS.

Notes: MAR blocks represent, to scale, MAR allocations but not the physical location, form, or material type within PF-4. Detail may not add to total due to rounding. The **Appendix** explains the programs in PF-4.

Abbreviations: AC, Analytical Chemistry; MC, Materials Characterization; MR&R, Materials Recycle and Recovery; PDC, Pit Disassembly and Conversion; PRP, Plutonium Recycle and Purification; RTBF, Readiness in Technical Base and Facilities.

---

[25] The Director of Los Alamos National Laboratory "paused" programmatic operations in PF-4 on June 27, 2013, in part to address nuclear criticality safety concerns. Letter from Peter Winokur, Chairman, Defense Nuclear Facilities Safety Board, to The Honorable Frank Klotz, Administrator, National Nuclear Security Administration, May 16, 2014, http://www.dnfsb.gov/sites/default/files/Board%20Activities/Letters/2014/ltr_2014516_24391.pdf. (Criticality safety refers to the risk that certain quantities and configurations of fissile material could support a nuclear chain reaction. The chain reaction would not result in a nuclear explosion but would release a flood of neutrons.) While the MAR allowance is fixed, actual MAR changes from day to day while PF-4 is in normal operating status, varying with the work being performed. PF-4 was in operating status on February 27, 2013.

allowance used by each program on that date. For example, Pu-238 work accounted for 24.5 percent of the 1,800 kg PE; pit fabrication, for 16.4 percent; and other tasks, for lesser amounts. The gray space, 21.5 percent, represents the PF-4 MAR allowance unused on February 27, 2013.

As noted, this analysis assumes that seismic upgrades increase PF-4 MAR to 2,600 kg PE. **Table 2** shows that amount of MAR to the same scale as **Table 1** and assumes that programs other than pit manufacturing use the MAR they used on February 27, 2013, for the foreseeable future. It shows that if the newly-available 800 kg PE of MAR and the unallocated MAR are both allocated to pit manufacturing and combined with the pit fabrication MAR, then 57.0 percent of the MAR in PF-4 would be available for pit work. (While the amount of MAR used by other tasks remains the same, the percentage of MAR they use is lower than in **Table 1** because each task accounts for a smaller fraction of the higher MAR allowance.)

Table 2. PF-4 MAR with Seismic Upgrades

Units in this graphic are kilograms of plutonium, not area
MAR allowance for PF-4 for this configuration is 2,600 kg of plutonium

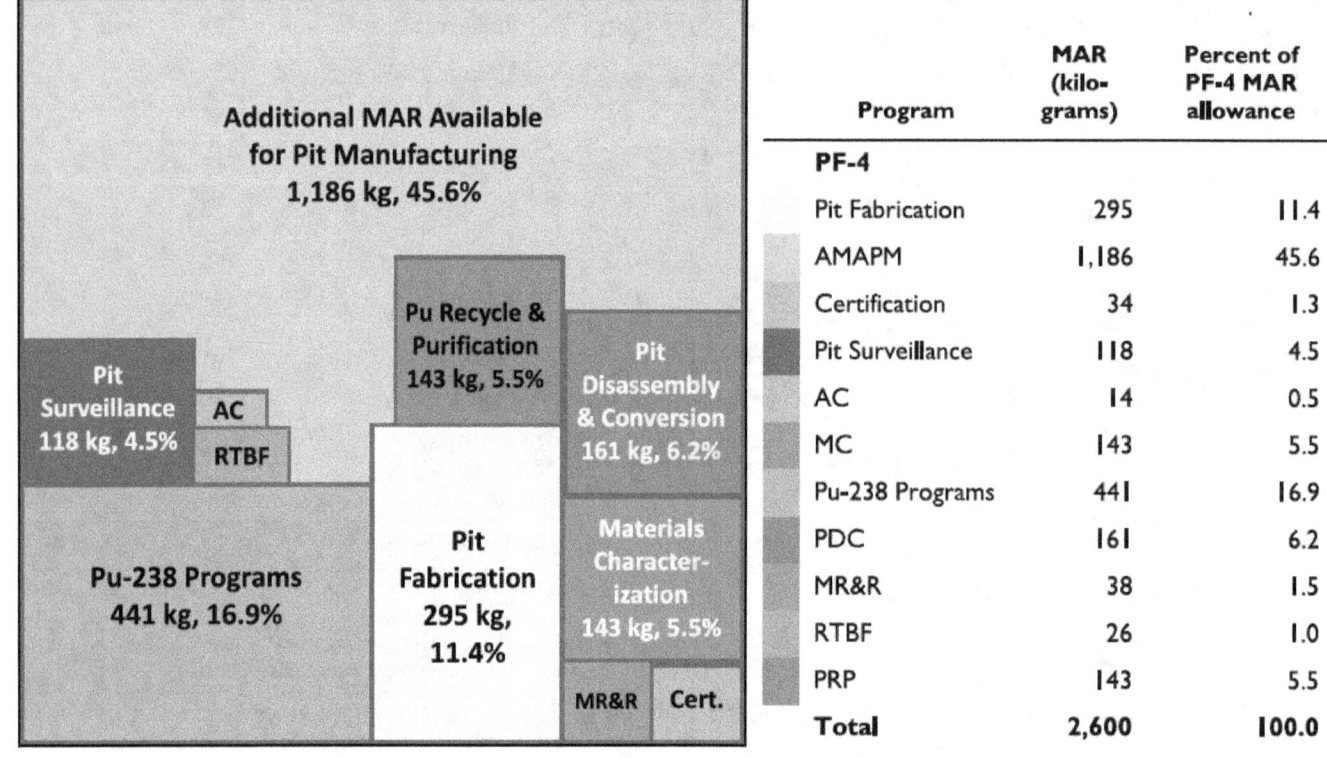

Program	MAR (kilograms)	Percent of PF-4 MAR allowance
PF-4		
Pit Fabrication	295	11.4
AMAPM	1,186	45.6
Certification	34	1.3
Pit Surveillance	118	4.5
AC	14	0.5
MC	143	5.5
Pu-238 Programs	441	16.9
PDC	161	6.2
MR&R	38	1.5
RTBF	26	1.0
PRP	143	5.5
Total	**2,600**	**100.0**

Source: Data provided by Los Alamos National Laboratory; graphic by CRS.

Notes: This graphic assumes that seismic improvements have raised the MAR allowance back to 2,600 kg, what it was before MAR was reduced due to seismic concerns, and that unallocated MAR is allocated to pit manufacture. MAR blocks represent, to scale, MAR allocations but not the physical location, form, or material type within PF-4. Detail may not add to total due to rounding. The **Appendix** explains the programs in PF-4.

Abbreviations: AC, Analytical Chemistry; AMAPM, Additional MAR Available for Pit Manufacturing; MC, Materials Characterization; MR&R, Materials Recycle and Recovery; PDC, Pit Disassembly and Conversion; PRP, Plutonium Recycle and Purification; RTBF, Readiness in Technical Base and Facilities.

If adding 800 kg of MAR is not sufficient to support 80 ppy, at least three other options would release more MAR. In discussing these options, it is important to recognize that MAR is not spread evenly across PF-4. While Pu-238 is only a small fraction of PF-4's radioactive material by weight, it is so radioactive that it is allocated 40 percent of PF-4's MAR allowance, though it did not use that much on February 27, 2013. Nor is MAR spread evenly within a program space, as discussed below.

Option 1, shown in **Table 3**, would use two modules. Plutonium Recycle and Purification (PRP) uses aqueous (plutonium dissolved in acid) processes and molten processes to recover pure plutonium from scrap or from retired pits by chemically removing impurities.[26] Module 1 would house aqueous processes from PRP, and Module 2 would house molten plutonium from Pit Fabrication and from PRP. (This would eliminate PRP within PF-4.) This option would move about 198 kg of MAR out of PF-4. On a scale using total PF-4 MAR (2,600 kg PE) as 100 percent, Module 1 would have 1.5 percent as much MAR as PF-4 and Module 2 would have 6.5 percent as much. MAR available in PF-4 for pit manufacturing would increase to 62.5 percent.

---

[26] Impurities include americium-241, a decay product of plutonium-239; neptunium-237, a decay product of americium-241; and various uranium isotopes that are decay products of various plutonium isotopes. In addition, some nonradioactive trace elements may have been introduced during previous manufacturing processes. All these would need to be eliminated, or at least reduced below a threshold, for the recovered plutonium to be suitable for use in pits.

Table 3. PF-4 MAR with Two Modules

Units in this graphic are kilograms of plutonium, not area
MAR allowance for PF-4 for this configuration is 2,600 kg of plutonium

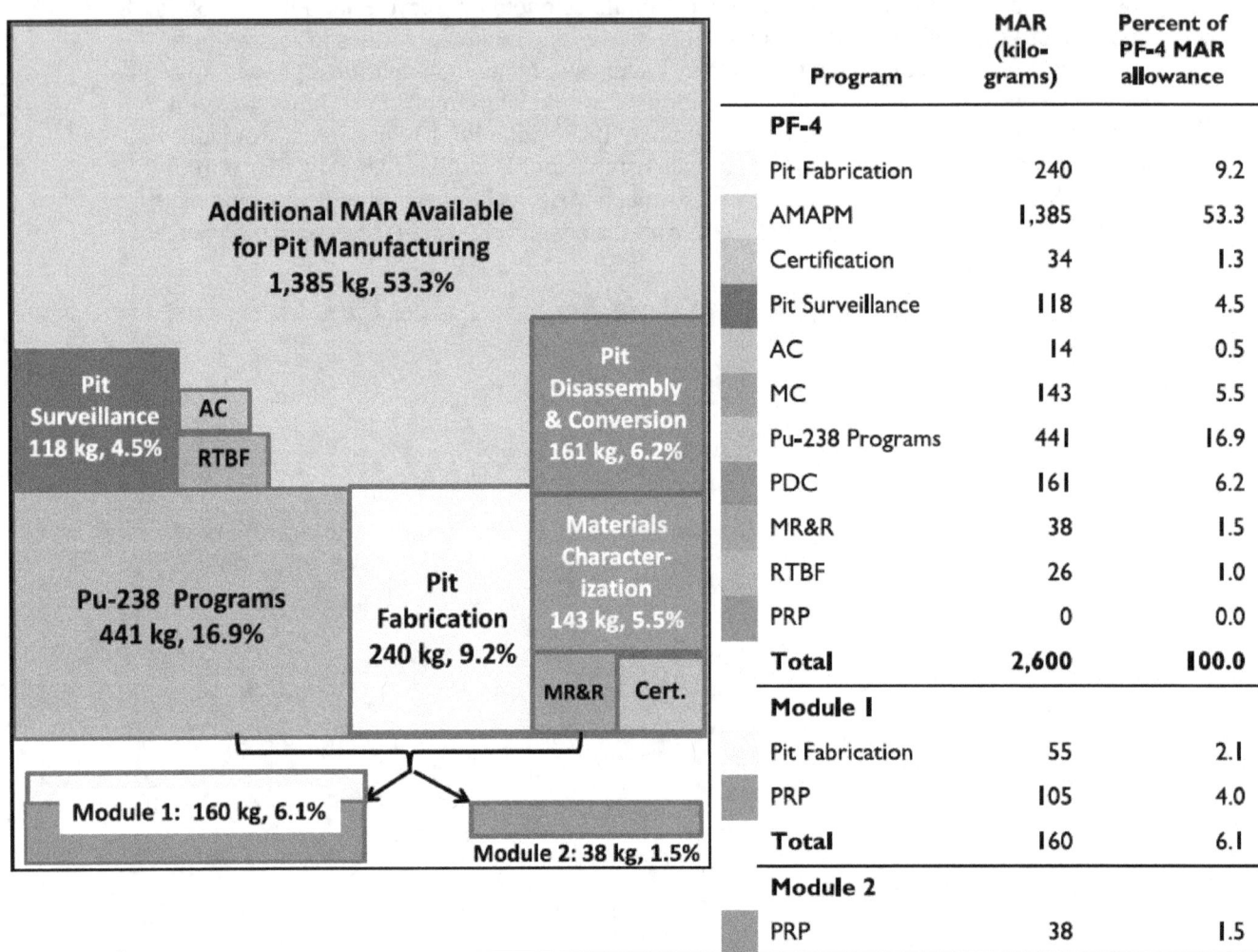

Program	MAR (kilo-grams)	Percent of PF-4 MAR allowance
PF-4		
Pit Fabrication	240	9.2
AMAPM	1,385	53.3
Certification	34	1.3
Pit Surveillance	118	4.5
AC	14	0.5
MC	143	5.5
Pu-238 Programs	441	16.9
PDC	161	6.2
MR&R	38	1.5
RTBF	26	1.0
PRP	0	0.0
Total	**2,600**	**100.0**
Module 1		
Pit Fabrication	55	2.1
PRP	105	4.0
Total	**160**	**6.1**
Module 2		
PRP	38	1.5

Source: Data provided by Los Alamos National Laboratory; graphic by CRS.

Notes: MAR blocks represent, to scale, MAR allocations but not the physical location, form, or material type within PF-4. MAR blocks outside PF-4 (modules) are drawn to the same scale as those inside. Module 1 is for Pit Fabrication (2/3) and Plutonium Recycle and Recovery (1/3); Module 2 is for Plutonium Recycle and Recovery. MAR not used for other programs is assumed to be allocated to pit manufacture. Detail may not add to total due to rounding.

Option 2 would move the Pu-238 MAR contained in 5,000 sf of PF-4 to one module, releasing 52 percent of the space of Pu-238 Programs and 91 percent of the MAR in those programs.[27] **Table**

---

[27] Los Alamos National Laboratory provided the following data. As of February 27, 2013, Pu-238 programs accounted for 440.68 kg of MAR in PF-4 and 9,600 square feet (sf) of space. Based on an analysis of the MAR by room in the Pu-238 area, Los Alamos calculated that a 5,000-sf module could accommodate 401.55 kg of Pu-238 MAR. By this calculation, therefore, the module would hold 91 percent of the MAR. While the amount of MAR varies from day to day, the fundamental point shown by the data is that MAR is not spread evenly across a program area.

4 shows this option. (Tables 2 through 5 are drawn to the same scale.) MAR available for repurposing would also be allocated to pit fabrication. Under Option 2, pit fabrication would be allocated 72.4 percent of the 2,600 kg PE of MAR in PF-4. This option requires half as many modules and releases twice the MAR as Option 1.

Table 4. PF-4 MAR with One Module

Units in this graphic are kilograms of plutonium, not area
MAR allowance for PF-4 for this configuration is 2,600 kg of plutonium

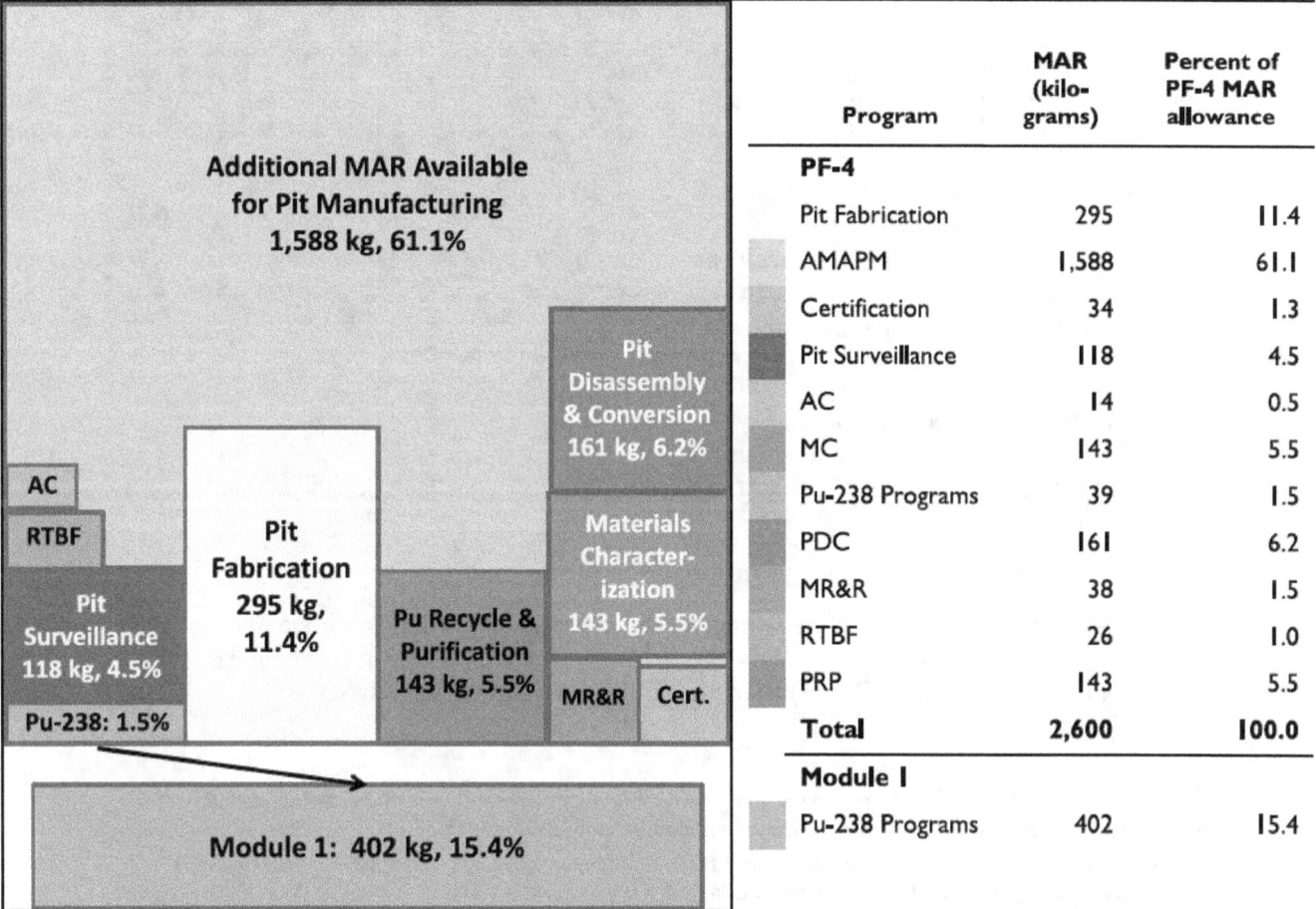

Program	MAR (kilo-grams)	Percent of PF-4 MAR allowance
PF-4		
Pit Fabrication	295	11.4
AMAPM	1,588	61.1
Certification	34	1.3
Pit Surveillance	118	4.5
AC	14	0.5
MC	143	5.5
Pu-238 Programs	39	1.5
PDC	161	6.2
MR&R	38	1.5
RTBF	26	1.0
PRP	143	5.5
Total	**2,600**	**100.0**
Module 1		
Pu-238 Programs	402	15.4

Source: Data provided by Los Alamos National Laboratory; graphic by CRS.

Notes: MAR blocks represent, to scale, MAR allocations but not the physical location, form, or material type within PF-4. MAR blocks outside PF-4 (modules) are drawn to the same scale as those inside. Module 1 is for Pit Fabrication (2/3) and Plutonium Recycle and Recovery (1/3); Module 2 is for Plutonium Recycle and Recovery. MAR not used for other programs is assumed to be allocated to pit manufacture. Detail may not add to total due to rounding. The **Appendix** explains the programs in PF-4.

Abbreviations: AC, Analytical Chemistry; AMAPM, Additional MAR Available for Pit Manufacturing; MC, Materials Characterization; MR&R, Materials Recycle and Recovery; PDC, Pit Disassembly and Conversion; PRP, Plutonium Recycle and Purification; RTBF, Readiness in Technical Base and Facilities.

Option 3 (not shown) would move all Pu-238 work to INL or SRS. This would free up all the MAR, vs. 91 percent for Option 2 and, more importantly, as shown in **Figure 4**, would free up 9,600 sf of space, vs. 5,000 for Option 2.

Increasing MAR Margin Without Major Construction

As with space, it may be possible to increase MAR margin without major construction. One approach is to strengthen PF-4 seismically to reduce the risk of building collapse through such steps as wrapping supporting columns in carbon fiber bonded with epoxy to strengthen them,[28] anchoring the wall more strongly to the ceiling, installing braces that tie columns to beams, building shear walls, and installing a drag strut on the roof of PF-4 (see **Figure 5**).[29]

Other steps could reduce the risk that plutonium would escape even if PF-4 collapsed; plutonium escaping in an accident causes dose, and dose is the key factor in determining the amount of MAR permitted. Actual or possible steps include:

Figure 5. PF-4 Roof Showing Drag Strut

Drag strut is circled

Source: Google Maps.

Notes: See footnote 29 for a description of drag struts.

- Installing in production areas containers designed to remain intact in a building collapse; plutonium in these containers is not "at risk" and is thus not MAR;

- Removing tons of combustible material from PF-4;[30] and

- Anchoring gloveboxes more strongly to the floor to reduce the likelihood that an earthquake would knock them over, exposing plutonium to the air, in which case a fire could generate plutonium oxide particles and release them into the atmosphere.[31]

---

[28] For a discussion of the use of this method in a large office building, see Mo Ehsani, "Fiber Reinforced Polymers: Seismic Retrofit of the McKinley Tower," *Structure Magazine,* Juny 2007, pp. 35-37.

[29] Los Alamos National Laboratory provided some of this information, email and telephone communications, May 2014. Drag struts "gather the lateral earthquake loads from a large area of a building—a roof or floor diaphragm, for example—and deliver them to a structural element, such as a shear wall, that can resist the force." Thor Matteson, "Lateral-Force Collectors for Seismic and Wind-Resistant Framing," Purdue Practical Engineering, October 2003, p. 1, https://engineering.purdue.edu/~jliu/courses/CE479/extras/Lateral-Force%20Collectors.pdf. A shear wall is "a rigid vertical diaphragm capable of transferring lateral forces from exterior walls, floors, and roofs to the ground foundation in a direction parallel to their planes. Examples are the reinforced-concrete wall or vertical truss. Lateral forces caused by wind, earthquake, and uneven settlement loads, in addition to the weight of structure and occupants, create powerful twisting (torsional) forces. These forces can literally tear (shear) a building apart. Reinforcing a frame by attaching or placing a rigid wall inside it maintains the shape of the frame and prevents rotation at the joints. Shear walls are especially important in high-rise buildings subject to lateral wind and seismic forces." "Shear Wall," *Encyclopedia Britannica,* Academic Edition, http://www.britannica.com/EBchecked/topic/539298/shear-wall.

[30] Los Alamos removed about 20 tons of combustible material from PF-4 between 2010 and 2012. Letter from Donald Cook, Deputy Administrator for Defense Programs, National Nuclear Security Administration, to Peter Winokur, Chairman, Defense Nuclear Facilities Safety Board, January 30, 2012, Enclosure 2, p. 1, http://www.dnfsb.gov/sites/default/files/Board%20Activities/Letters/2012/ltr_2012130_18446_0.pdf.

[31] This work is underway in PF-4. See Figure 16 in CRS Report R43406, *U.S. Nuclear Weapon "Pit" Production Options for Congress*, by Jonathan E. Medalia

---

Options for Analytical Chemistry

Figure 6. Preparing a Sample for an Analytical Chemistry Instrument

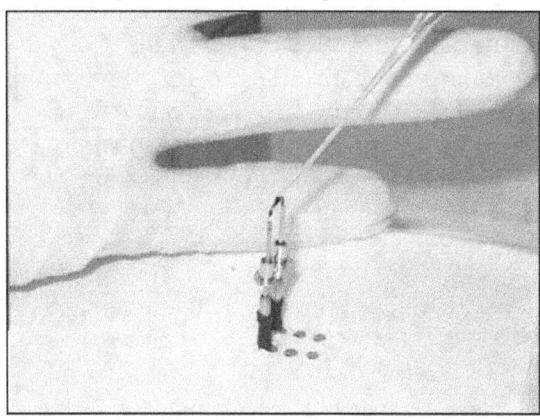

Source: Los Alamos National Laboratory.

Unlike pit manufacturing, AC involves little MAR because it uses tiny samples, such as a few milligrams of plutonium dissolved in a small amount of acid, as **Figure 6** shows. But AC involves much more space per unit MAR than does pit fabrication because each laboratory instrument is housed in a glovebox or hood that might occupy a dozen square feet of space. Many analyses must be performed for each individual pit, and the number of instruments and their housing increase in tandem with manufacturing capacity. Producing 80 ppy would require increasing AC capacity.

This requirement comes from two sources. First, at LANL, most pit-related AC is performed in the CMR building; as noted, NNSA plans to halt programmatic operations there "in approximately 2019." Given NNSA's plan to achieve a 30-ppy capacity by FY2026, work currently done in CMR would have to be performed elsewhere. Second, producing 80 ppy would require additional AC, as AC must be performed on multiple samples for each pit, and increasing manufacturing capacity would require more equipment, more space, and more MAR for AC.

Finding enough space and MAR for AC should be simpler than for pit manufacture because more options are readily available to meet requirements for AC than for pit manufacture. According to DOD, "At the height of the Cold War, the Department of Energy's Rocky Flats Plant produced between 1,000 and 2,000 pits per year."[32] The plutonium for each pit required AC. Because currently-anticipated rates do not approach that level, the nuclear weapons complex has a considerable amount of excess space and MAR suitable for AC. This capacity resides at several buildings in the complex, including Building 332 at Lawrence Livermore National Laboratory (LLNL), F/H Laboratory and Building 773-A at SRS, and the Radiological Laboratory-Utility-Office Building (RLUOB) at LANL. Each of these facilities would apparently have enough floor space and MAR allowance to conduct the AC needed to support manufacture of 80 ppy, PF-4 might perform some additional AC for higher-MAR work, such as sample preparation (which takes several-gram samples from larger pieces of plutonium) and certain analyses. **Figure 7** shows these options. In addition, R&D may reduce MAR requirements. For example, LANL is validating an AC system that may require a sample size of 1.5 mg of WGPu instead of 225 mg.[33]

---

[32] U.S. Department of Defense. "Assessment of Nuclear Weapon Pit Production Requirements," January 2014, p. 2.

[33] Craig Leasure and Matthew Nuckols, *Los Alamos Initial Response for Maintaining Capabilities with Deferral of the CMRR Nuclear Facility Project,* Los Alamos National Laboratory, LA-CP-12-00470, April 16, 2012, p. 47. This document is Unclassified Controlled Nuclear Information, but this sentence is unclassified.

At issue are whether all AC should be done at LANL and, if not, how much AC should be done there and how much at another site. Not at issue is that LANL would need the *capability* to perform all AC tasks even if it did not have the *capacity* to perform AC for 80 ppy. The case for having a second site perform some of the AC needed for 80 ppy while maintaining the full suite of AC capabilities at LANL is:

- LANL is primarily a laboratory, and AC for 80 ppy would be on an industrial scale. LANL would gain little if any technical competence by conducting AC for 80 ppy vs., say, 40.

- It may be difficult to provide enough MAR and floor space at LANL for the AC for 80 ppy, especially with RLUOB's current MAR limit of 26 grams WGPu.

- LANL and a second site could cross-check the accuracy of each other's AC measurements and processes from time to time. LANL and LLNL have for decades, since before the end of nuclear testing, held that peer review is essential in developing or maintaining weapons and leads each lab to probe for flaws in the other lab's analyses, thus increasing confidence in the results. A similar argument could apply to peer review of AC.

- A second site could accommodate a surge in AC needs or provide a backup in case AC operations at LANL were suspended or disrupted.

- A second site would provide another source of technicians trained for plutonium AC.

Several factors argue for keeping all the AC at LANL.

- It might cost more to perform AC at two sites rather than one, though it is impossible to know without the data.

- A second site would necessitate shipping many plutonium samples per year from LANL to another site, which would increase the risk of an accident and could cause public concern.

- It might be beneficial to have all plutonium AC technicians at one site so they would have the same training and operate according to the same formal and informal procedures.

- Concentrating as much plutonium work as possible at LANL would strengthen its position as the nation's plutonium center.

Figure 7. Analytical Chemistry: Requirements and Options

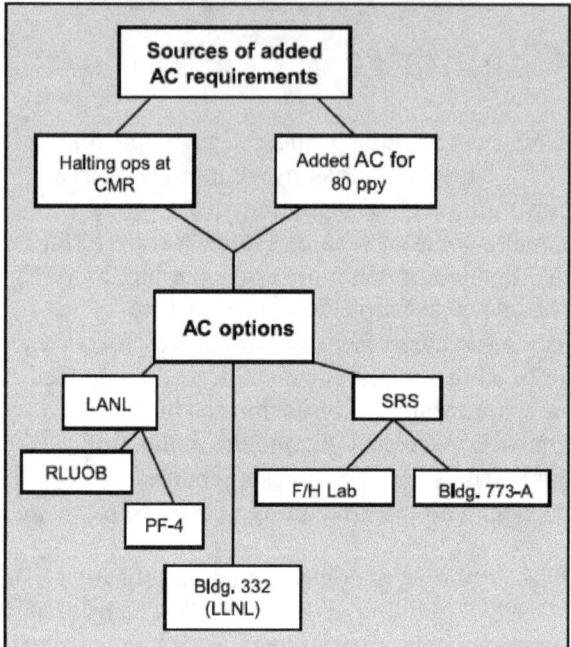

Source: CRS.

While SRS and LLNL could both do this work, their facilities presumably have different capacities and would require different upgrades to support whatever level of AC was required. Data on the MAR and space requirements, and the cost of the LANL, LLNL, and SRS options, would be needed to provide a basis for decision.

A New NNSA Path Forward on Analytical Chemistry[34]

The option of having LLNL or SRS conduct a substantial fraction of the AC needed to support manufacture of 80 ppy must be evaluated in light of a revised path forward for AC that NNSA developed in June 2014. Based on an initial analysis by Los Alamos National Laboratory, NNSA determined that the combination of PF-4 and RLUOB with a higher plutonium limit, if properly equipped, could likely conduct all the AC needed to support manufacture of 80 ppy. NNSA further found that RLUOB would have sufficient space for the needed equipment. The planning for this approach will be conducted by personnel from NNSA headquarters (including the Office of Defense Programs, the Office of General Counsel, and staff specializing in construction and in National Environmental Policy Act issues), NNSA's Los Alamos Field Office, and Los Alamos National Laboratory over the summer and fall of 2014 to understand the costs and benefits of this approach.

A Radiological Facility like RLUOB is permitted to hold up to 38.6 grams of plutonium-239 equivalent (Pu-239E), or 26 grams of WGPu. Radiological Facilities do not require stringent safety or security measures because the dose to onsite or offsite personnel in the event of a worst-case accident would be very low. In contrast, a Hazard Category (HC) 3 facility can hold between 38.6 grams and 2,610 grams of Pu-239E, or about 26 to 1,760 grams of WGPu. NNSA considered several options for raising the MAR limit in RLUOB. One option was to retrofit the building by adding various safety upgrades to make it HC-3 at the highest level (1760 grams WGPu). That option would have been costly and time-consuming and was not necessary for conducting AC work required. Another option was to create a "Hazard Category 4," splitting off the lower part of the HC-3 range into a separate category, with the upper bound, say, 900 grams Pu-239E. That option, however, would have necessitated a revision of 10 CFR 830, Nuclear Safety Management, which would have required an extended period for rulemaking and would likely have impacted many other DOE facilities.

The various limits on plutonium are based on the dose to onsite workers and offsite personnel that a worst-case accident could be expected to cause, and the requirements for a building depend on dose. There are myriad other regulations, all of which come together in a document called a Documented Safety Analysis, or DSA, which is tailored to each building and specifies the amount of radioactive material the building can hold and still remain below the dose thresholds set by DOE Orders in the event of a worst-case accident. While each building in the Hazard Category system requires a DSA, a Radiological Facility, such as RLUOB, does not because the amount of radioactive material is so small. Therefore, to increase the amount of WGPu in RLUOB above 26 grams, NNSA would have to prepare a DSA to operate RLUOB as an HC-3 facility. NNSA calculated that RLUOB, with 400 grams WGPu, could likely be operated as HC-3 without significant facility modifications: because of modern building features in RLUOB, NNSA

---

[34] Information in this section, excepting footnote 38, was provided by Don Cook, Deputy Administrator for Defense Programs, NNSA, and Michael Thompson, Assistant Deputy Administrator, Major Modernization Programs, NNSA, telephone conversation, July 7, 2014.

calculated that the dose from the increased material in a worst-case accident would still be below the dose thresholds set by DOE Orders.

Operating RLUOB as an HC-3 facility would not require congressional approval. Instead, congressional oversight would come through the normal reviews associated with the Chemistry and Metallurgy Research Replacement (CMRR) line item construction project. This line item remains open. It would fund actions that would accomplish the tasks proposed for CMRR-Nuclear Facility (NF), which NNSA stated in its FY2013 request were "plutonium chemistry, plutonium physics, and storage of special nuclear materials."[35] However, CMRR-NF was "deferr[ed] … for at least five years" in the FY2013 budget request on cost grounds.[36] NNSA plans to include funds for two subprojects in the CMRR line item construction project beginning with the FY2016 request. One is adding new AC equipment to RLUOB so it can perform AC to support 80 ppy; this would be "RLUOB Equipment Installation 2," or REI-2; the initial REI provided equipment for a much smaller amount of AC. AC equates to plutonium chemistry. The other involves PF-4: decontaminating some rooms, removing some old gloveboxes, and installing new materials characterization (MC)[37] equipment; this is "Plutonium Equipment Installation," or PEI. PEI would support MC, and relates to plutonium physics. A separate activity, not part of the CMRR project, is removing excess special nuclear materials from the storage vault in PF-4, work that has been underway for some years.[38]

As a result, these three elements would permit NNSA to perform all the tasks planned for CMRR-NF, the cost of which was projected in the FY2012 budget request to be between $3,710 million and $5,860 million.[39] While there are no cost estimates for NNSA's path forward, it would cost substantially less than CMRR-NF because it would avoid building a large plutonium facility.

NNSA requested FY2015 funds for the AC and MC subprojects as part of the Program Readiness component of Readiness in Technical Base and Facilities (RTBF), which in turn is a component of NNSA's Weapons Activities account.[40] While the House Appropriations Committee recommended including these funds as RTBF Construction, using the CMRR line item to fund these projects is consistent with the committee's recommendation:

> *04-D-125, Chemistry and Metallurgy Research (CMR) Replacement Project, LANL.*—The Committee recommends $35,700,000, instead of providing funds for these activities under

---

[35] U.S. Department of Energy. Office of Chief Financial Officer. *FY 2013 Congressional Budget Request,* Volume 1, National Nuclear Security Administration, DOE/CF-0071, February 2012, p. 185. Special nuclear materials are essentially uranium enriched in the isotope 235 and plutonium.

[36] Ibid.

[37] Materials characterization measures bulk properties of plutonium, such as tensile strength, magnetic susceptibility, grain structure, and surface characteristics, and uses samples on the order of a fraction of a gram to tens of grams. In contrast, analytical chemistry, which measures such chemical properties of plutonium as impurities and isotopic composition, typically uses samples on the order of milligrams.

[38] Much material can be removed from the vault. As of early 2012, approximately 30 percent of the PF-4 vault space was "occupied by material of use to programs," 66 percent was occupied by "materials of no current value to the programs," and 4 percent was "available space." Leasure and Nuckols, *Los Alamos Initial Response for Maintaining Capabilities with Deferral of the CMRR Nuclear Facility Project,* p. 77. This document is Unclassified Controlled Nuclear Information, but the preceding sentence is unclassified.

[39] U.S. Department of Energy. Office of Chief Financial Officer. *FY 2012 Congressional Budget Request,* Volume 1, National Nuclear Security Administration, DOE/CF-0057, February 2011, p. 237.

[40] U.S. Department of Energy. Office of Chief Financial Officer. *FY 2015 Congressional Budget Request.* Volume 1, National Nuclear Security Administration. DOE/CF-0096, March 2014, p. 213.

Program Readiness as in the budget request. This approach is consistent with the Committee's previous direction to the NNSA to carry out all CMR replacement activities in accordance with DOE Order 413.3B, rather than within operations funding where there is little transparency or accountability for delivering these activities on time and within budget. While the capacity and amount of process equipment needed may be evolving due to changing programmatic requirements for plutonium, the scope of the additional work being requested is consistent with the original mission need to provide analytic chemistry and material characterization space in a different facility than the legacy CMR building. Similarly, PF-4 reconfiguration activities are also appropriate to be conducted as part of the original CMR Replacement project so long as they are limited to re-equipping lab space for capabilities that were previously housed in the legacy CMR building. Construction of new modular facilities and installation of equipment within PF-4 to establish enhanced pit production capabilities are not sufficiently related to the original mission need of the existing project, and the Committee does not support the inclusion of these activities as subprojects within the existing CMR replacement project.[41]

REI-2 and PEI would also permit NNSA to exit the CMR building, a long-time goal of NNSA for several reasons:

- a fault runs underneath the building;

- CMR was built to the seismic standards of the late 1940s, so it is much more vulnerable to collapse in an earthquake than is RLUOB, placing its workers at heightened risk; and

- studies have found it to be "decrepit" and "structurally unsound," as noted under "Terminology."

NNSA points out that—comparing the quantity of plutonium, the age, and the structural integrity of the two buildings—having 9 kg of plutonium in CMR, as at present, poses a much greater risk than having 400 grams of plutonium in RLUOB.

If NNSA is able to implement its path forward, LANL could perform all the AC needed to support manufacture of up to 80 ppy. In that case, the key question for AC would be how much, if any, AC one or more sites other than LANL should perform.

Decisions Require Data

The foregoing discussion shows how much additional space and MAR various construction options would make available for pit manufacturing, and points out that various non-construction options would also increase space and MAR margins. LANL has provided data from which this report calculated how much MAR and space various options would make available. The data, however, cannot indicate which options, if any, would provide *enough* margin because data on space and MAR *requirements* are also needed to calculate margin. It might turn out that once seismic improvements are made, PF 4 would have enough space and MAR margin for 80 ppy, or that moving Pu-238 programs to a module might free up enough MAR but not enough space for 80 ppy, or that moving Pu-238 programs to another site would suffice. (Other factors may enter

---

[41] U.S. Congress, House Committee on Appropriations, *Energy and Water Development Appropriations Bill, 2015*, report to accompany H.R. 4923, 113th Cong., 2nd sess., June 20, 2014, H.Rept. 113-486 (Washington: GPO, 2014), pp. 135-136.

into feasibility as well, such as the condition of a building.) But without data for space and MAR needed to manufacture 80 ppy, one cannot know which options are infeasible, which provide excess capacity and thus entail excess cost, and which are "just right."

Regarding AC, the discussion shows that there are multiple options to provide AC capacity, and highlights the issue of whether all AC should be done at LANL and, if not, how much AC should be done there and how much at another site. But without data on such matters as building condition and cost for any required upgrades and equipment, it is not possible to determine the relative merits of the options.

Figure 8 shows a notional decision sequence for downselecting pit manufacturing options. After defining options meriting consideration, the first question is, Which options are feasible? It would be simple to compare data on the required MAR and space, once they become available, against the amount of MAR and space released by each option to see which options provide a positive margin. Non-feasible options would not merit further consideration. The next step would be to estimate the cost of the feasible options and decide which are affordable. These data are needed to eliminate unaffordable options, which is important before planning begins because high cost has caused the demise of several nuclear weapons complex projects. Finally, having downselected to options that are feasible and affordable, one would compare those options against other possible criteria in order to make a final choice. Not shown in the figure is that MAR and space margins may change over time, as **Figure 1** shows; such changes may make currently-feasible options infeasible, and vice versa.

Figure 8. Notional Decision Sequence for Downselecting Pit Manufacturing Options

Options	A	B	C	D	E	F	G	H	I	J
Enough MAR?	YES	NO	YES	NO	YES	YES	NO	NO	YES	YES
Enough space?	NO	NO	YES	YES	YES	YES	NO	YES	YES	NO
Feasible set			C		E	F			I	
Cost ($B)			1.5		0.9	1.4			8.3	
Affordable?			YES		YES	YES			NO	
Feasible and affordable set			C		E	F				
Compare against other criteria			fair		poor	excellent				
Final selection					PROCEED					

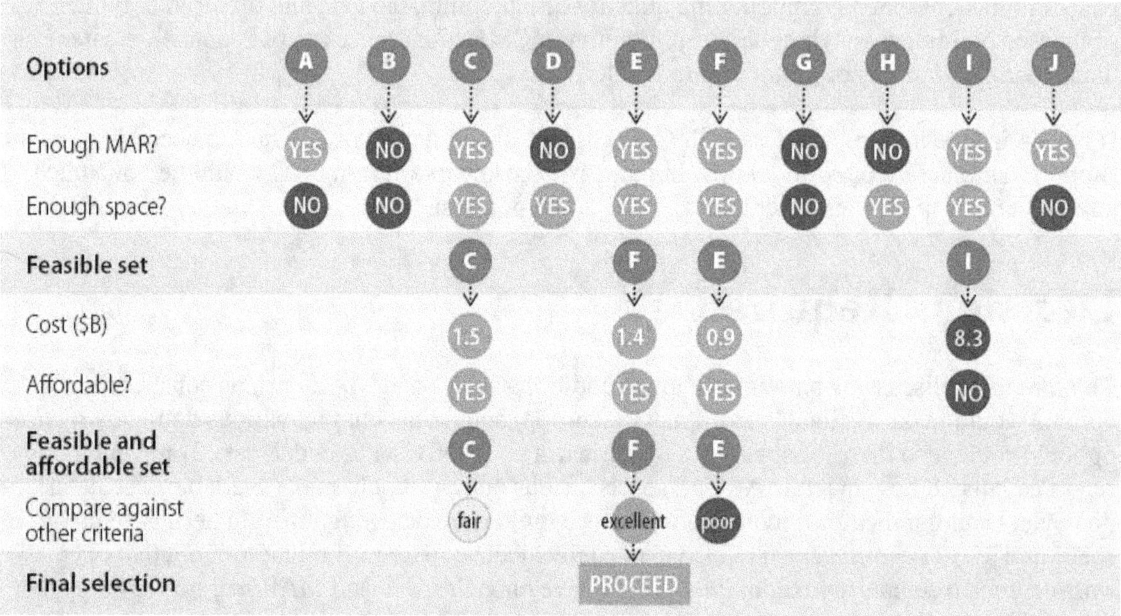

Source: CRS.

Note: Options are notional, and do not represent any specific options.

Questions That Can Only Be Answered with Data

Congress would need data on MAR margin, space margin, and cost for various pit manufacturing options in order to best determine which options are feasible and affordable. The following questions highlight how these data could support decisionmaking.

Questions Requiring Data on MAR and Space

Questions such as the following can only be answered with data on how much MAR and space suffice for pit manufacturing and supporting AC for 80 ppy:

- Once certain seismic upgrades are completed, is there expected to be enough MAR margin for PF-4 to accommodate the added MAR needed to manufacture 80 ppy?

- As of 2012, 4,700 sf was available for immediate repurposing in PF-4. How much space is available now? Is that space, plus the 12,000 sf for pit fabrication, plus space for other pit-related tasks, enough to manufacture 80 ppy?

- If there is enough space and MAR margin in PF-4 for 80 ppy, is there a need to move any pit fabrication work (such as hemishell casting), Pu-238 work, or any other high-MAR work out of PF-4, whether to modules or to another site?

- If the MAR allowance in PF-4 is not sufficient to accommodate manufacture of 80 ppy, by how much would it have to be raised to do so? Could that be done, and if so what would the project entail?

- MAR is not evenly distributed across space. As noted, 91 percent of Pu-238 MAR was at one point concentrated in 5,000 sf of the 9,600 sf that Pu-238 Programs occupy in PF-4. (MAR usage within PF-4 changes from day to day; the MAR figure is for February 27, 2013.) Would moving this MAR into a 5,000-sf module make enough MAR and space available in PF-4 for manufacture of 80 ppy?

- Moving all Pu-238 work to INL or SRS would release a little more MAR but another 4,600 sf, as compared to a module. Would that release enough MAR and space in PF-4 to permit manufacture of 80 ppy?

- Would one module release enough MAR and space in PF-4 for pit manufacture? (This assumes that the immediately-repurposable space in PF-4 would also be used for pit manufacture.) If yes, would that be the case if pit casting were moved to the module, or if Pu-238 were moved to the module?

- Space in PF-4 is precious, as PF-4 is the only place in the United States that performs high-MAR, high-security work on plutonium and can manufacture pits. Unused space therefore represents opportunity for plutonium work forgone. Would moving 5,000 sf of Pu-238 work and 5,000 sf of pit casting equipment to two modules create unused space in PF-4? Would moving the entire Pu-238 line, 9,600 sf, to another site have the same result? Or would the released space be needed to accommodate added equipment needed to manufacture 80 ppy?

- At present, RLUOB is permitted to have 26 grams of WGPu MAR for AC, which is not nearly enough to perform the AC for 80 ppy. If this limit remains in place, how much more MAR and space would be needed for AC at LLNL or SRS?

- If the MAR limit for RLUOB is increased to 400 grams of WGPu for AC, how much more MAR and space, if any, would be needed for AC at LLNL or SRS?

Questions Requiring Data on Cost

- If the 26-gram limit is retained for RLUOB, would it be less costly to perform the remaining AC at LLNL or at SRS?

- What would it cost to enable RLUOB to hold 400 grams WGPu?

- If RLUOB could hold 400 grams of WGPu but that did not provide sufficient space for AC for 80 ppy, would it be less costly to perform the remaining AC at LLNL or at SRS?

- LANL is conducting projects to bolster the seismic robustness of PF-4, which may increase PF-4's MAR allowance from 1,800 to 2,600 kg PE (or more or less). If 2,600 kg PE is not enough MAR, could additional projects raise the MAR allowance enough to accommodate manufacture of 80 ppy, and what would they cost?

- LANL maintains that each successive module should cost less than the one before it, as lessons learned should drive down costs. On the other hand, it is possible that some lessons learned would lead to increased costs. What is the first module estimated to cost? The second?

- How sensitive is the cost of pit manufacturing to capacity, and what tradeoffs might a sensitivity analysis reveal? As a hypothetical example, if it cost an additional several billion dollars to move from 70 to 80 ppy, would it be worth spending the added money?

- Would it be less costly to move Pu-238 or hemishell casting to a module?

- Would it be less costly to move Pu-238 to INL, SRS, or a newly-built module?

Conclusion

In deciding how to proceed on pit manufacture, Congress would likely want to know if there is enough space margin and MAR margin for 80 ppy. Margin, the available resource (space or MAR) minus the required resource, must be greater than zero. Available space and MAR are known, as of certain dates, as this report shows. But space and MAR required for 80 ppy have not been rigorously calculated. Congress may choose to direct NNSA to provide these two numbers.

Once these numbers become available, Congress would face three decisions:

- For pit manufacturing, is there currently enough margin for space and MAR in PF-4? If not, what can be done to provide it?

- Once enough margin for space and margin for MAR are provided for pit manufacturing, what steps can be taken to maintain these margins over decades in the face of uncertainties?

- Space and MAR margins are not at issue for analytical chemistry because considerable excess space and MAR exist at other sites in the nuclear weapons complex. At issue: How much AC should be done at LANL, what is needed to make the space and MAR at LANL sufficient to support that amount of AC, and how much, if any, AC should be done at other sites?

Appendix. Plutonium Tasks in PF-4

This appendix explains the tasks included in the diagrams of PF-4 and, in so doing, explains what PF-4 does.

Analytical Chemistry (AC) analyzes plutonium samples taken from each pit at various stages in its manufacture. AC measures the isotopic composition of the plutonium and the amount of alloying materials and impurities a sample contains. AC typically uses samples on the order of milligrams.

Certification: Before a pit type can be accepted into the stockpile, it must be certified as acceptable for war reserve use. This involves validating weapons codes, among other things. Validation, in turn, draws on experimental data. PF-4 supports some of these experiments, such as by preparing samples for analytical chemistry and materials characterization and preparing test items for experiments at the Nevada National Security Site that do not produce a nuclear yield.

Materials Characterization (MC): MC measures bulk properties of plutonium, such as tensile strength, magnetic susceptibility, grain structure, and surface characteristics. Such properties must be determined in order to certify pit design, maintain process control, address process anomalies, and examine the condition of newly-manufactured pits and pits from the stockpile. MC typically uses samples on the order of a fraction of a gram to tens of grams.

Materials Recycle and Recovery (MR&R): MR&R examines containers of plutonium in PF-4 that are to be sent to WIPP for permanent disposition. If the containers have deteriorated, MR&R repackages the plutonium in new containers.

Pit Disassembly and Conversion: This area of PF-4 houses ARIES (Advanced Recovery and Integrated Extraction System), which converts excess pits to plutonium oxide (a powder) and places it in special containers for long-term storage.

Pit Fabrication involves, among other things, casting "hemishells" (half-pits) of plutonium, machining the cast hemishells to remove excess material, welding two together to form a pit, and inspecting the finished pit with x-ray imaging, physical measurements, etc., to ensure it meets specifications.

Pit Surveillance: Ever since the beginning of the nuclear weapons program, NNSA and its predecessor organizations have monitored the condition of nuclear weapons using a variety of techniques. Pits are monitored at Pantex Plant (TX) and PF-4. PF-4 monitoring techniques include taking physical measurements, checking for release of gases that may indicate deterioration of the pit, examining pits for corrosion, and taking pits apart to perform AC and MC on samples of the plutonium. While Pantex can perform some of these tasks, pits can be disassembled only at PF-4.

Plutonium-238 (Pu-238) Programs: Pu-238 is the heat source for radioisotope power systems (RPS) for space probes, and has military applications as well. It is manufactured by bombarding rods of neptunium-237 with neutrons in a nuclear reactor. It undergoes radioactive decay much more rapidly than does Pu-239, producing uranium and other impurities. As a result, old Pu-238 must be purified before it can be used. PF-4 receives Pu-238, removes the impurities through chemical processes, and makes plutonium oxide, which it presses into capsules. It mates some capsules with other equipment to make RPSs for military applications, and sends other capsules to Idaho National Laboratory, which does the same to make RPSs for space probes.

Plutonium Recycle and Purification (PR&P): This area recovers plutonium from scrap plutonium (such as from lathe turnings, pits scrapped for not meeting standards, or retired pits) for use in weapons and other programs. The scraps are dissolved in acid. Plutonium is then precipitated out of solution as plutonium oxalate, and is then roasted to produce plutonium oxide. A further process removes plutonium that remains in the acid. This area also recovers and purifies plutonium using high-temperature chemical processes.

Readiness in Technical Base and Facilities (RTBF): RTBF is NNSA's program for operating the nuclear weapons complex and maintaining its infrastructure. Within PF-4, RTBF space is used for functions that support multiple programs, such as shipping and receiving, waste management, and material control and accountability.

Author Contact Information

Jonathan E. Medalia
Specialist in Nuclear Weapons Policy
jmedalia@crs.loc.gov, 7-7632

Acknowledgments

Drew Kornreich of Los Alamos National Laboratory provided the space and MAR data used in this report. Sandra Edwards, Claudia Guidi, and Amber Wilhelm, all of CRS, provided extensive and invaluable graphics and formatting support. Brett Kniss, Drew Kornreich, and Craig Leasure, all of Los Alamos National Laboratory, Greg Mello of Los Alamos Study Group, and Don Cook and Michael Thompson, both of NNSA, were consulted in the preparation of this report.

www.ingramcontent.com/pod-product-compliance
Lightning Source LLC
Chambersburg PA
CBHW080733290526
45790CB00008B/3173